Chic Sweats

ALSO BY
SISTAHS OF HARLEM
Carmen Webber and
. . Carmia Marshall . .

Denim Mania:
25 Stylish Ways to Transform Your Jeans

T-Shirt Makeovers:
20 Transformations for Fabulous Fashions

22 Ways to Transform and Restyle Your Sweatshirts

Chic Sweats

sistahs of harlem
CARMEN WEBBER
AND CARMIA MARSHALL

ST. MARTIN'S GRIFFIN
NEW YORK

PHOTOGRAPHS BY DERRICK GOMEZ
ILLUSTRATIONS BY CARMEN WEBBER
BOOK DESIGN BY DEBORAH KERNER

Library of Congress Cataloging-in-Publication Data

Webber, Carmen.
    Chic sweats : 22 ways to transform and restyle your sweatshirts / Carmen Webber and Carmia Marshall.—1st ed.
        p. cm.
    Includes index.
ISBN-13: 978-0-312-37861-5
ISBN-10: 0-312-37861-0
1. Sweatshirts. 2. Clothing and dress—Remaking. I. Marshall, Carmia II. Title.

TT649.W34 2009
746.9'.2—dc22

First Edition: September 2009
10 9 8 7 6 5 4 3 2 1

contents

Introduction

We love comfort. More and more, we are taking casual pieces and transforming them into style-conscious apparel. Just like the T-shirt and blue jeans, the sweatshirt is embracing a new image. Comfy sweatshirts are now embellished with luxurious crystals. Hand-painted designs and intricate silk screening have found a new home.

Pop stars such as T.I. and Ciara take center stage in souped-up sweatshirts, both on the red carpet as well as in their fabulous blinged-out music videos. To wear a hooded sweatshirt with a cinched waist and leg-o'-mutton sleeves is fashion forward.

The sweatshirt is the new style staple. It's the next big thing!

Happy Sewing!!!

carmen:

O f course, I own tons of sweatshirts! Oversize sweatshirts hold a permanent place in my closet. These days, I am ripping my old sweatshirts out of my closet and creating hot threads that place me in the forefront of any fashion crowd! Often, I would wear a baby tee in the winter. I would feel a little cold and need an extra layering piece. I want to wear something cutting edge and fun—like my T-shirt and jeans—yet warm and comfortable. It only makes sense to transform my sweatshirts into a new haute couture item.

Chic Sweats will teach you how to transform vintage sweatshirts into beautiful new garments and accessories. Each project is easy to make, following our step-by-step instructions accompanied by detailed illustrations.

Carmen Webber

carmia:

I came across a recent article in the *New York Times* by Ruth La Ferla. The article was about the expanding market for fashion sweatshirts! Amazing. We want to look and feel great in a supercomfortable manner. The day of "looking good is painful" is disappearing. Comfort and style are synonymous; once-frumpy sweats are firmly in vogue.

I see fashion sweats everywhere. The sweatshirt is the finishing touch of casual urban chic. As with any new trend, these flamboyant sweatshirts are costly.

The once-ultracasual sweat has evolved. There was a time when I would lounge in my sweats carelessly. Like a couch potato, I'd put my feet up, grab a bag of chips, and lose myself in one of my favorite novels, *The Alchemist*. To relax in sweats was second nature.

Now I find myself reaching for my souped-up hoodie to funk up an otherwise ordinary ensemble. I am not just limited to my sweatshirts but also have my sweatpants. They have adopted a new level of sophistication. Cargo sweats and wide-leg capri sweats are parading the streets like the best fashions on the runway. Just when I thought wearing sweats was dowdy, the glamour-sweat movement debuted.

Carmia Marshall

sweat
BASICS

Getting Started

Here is everything you need to know to turn your sweatshirts into fashion, from measuring and marking, to cutting, sewing, and embellishing. With our easy-to-follow instructions and step-by-step illustrations, you can master these basics even if you've never sewn before. More experienced sewers should review this section also. We give you a lot of tips for sewing sweatshirt fabrics, and have adapted various traditional sewing techniques for working with these fabrics specifically.

Probably the most valuable piece of advice we can give you about creating fashion-sweat styles is: Take your time. Patience is the single most important ingredient in achieving the result you want.

This section will cover the fundamental tools and techniques you'll need for every project in this book. It will be a great reference as you are working on the projects.

Supplies and Equipment

Proper tools equal great results. The right tool for the right task saves you time and endless frustration, and helps you create pieces that fit well and look professionally made.

Some basic tools and supplies are needed for every project, others are either needed only for some projects or, while not absolutely essential, would be very helpful to have on hand.

FABRIC SCISSORS: You should have a pair of good-quality scissors designed to cut fabric, and use them *only* for cutting fabric. (Cutting paper or other materials with your fabric scissors will dull the blades and make your sweat fabric much more difficult to cut.)

HANDSEWING NEEDLES: We recommend you purchase a package of assorted handsewing needles, which includes sharps, darners, embroidery, tapestry, and chenille needles in a variety of sizes.

HEAVY-DUTY STRAIGHT PINS: Quilting pins are especially good because they are long and have a ball head. But any long pin will work.

IRON AND IRONING BOARD: Good pressing is the key to making a fabulous garment.

MARKING DEVICES: You can mark with tailor's chalk, tailor's pen or pencil, or dressmaker's tracing paper and a tracing wheel. Select two different colors of tracing paper to contrast with dark and light fabrics.

MEASURING DEVICES: You'll need a cloth tape measure and straight and (ideally) curved-edged rulers. We think clear patternmaking rulers work best, but any ruler or yardstick will do. And if you don't have a French curve, your tape measure is flexible enough to form a curved line.

SEWING MACHINE AND SERGER (OR OVERLOCK MACHINE): You don't have to use a sewing machine or serger to execute our projects. But if you know how to use one, it will cut your time investment in half. Use a sewing machine needle designed for medium-to heavyweight knits (14–18 pt).

THREAD: For general hand- or machine sewing, all-purpose sewing thread—cotton-covered, polyester or mercerized cotton—works beautifully. You can also use buttonhole thread for buttonholes and to attach buttons.

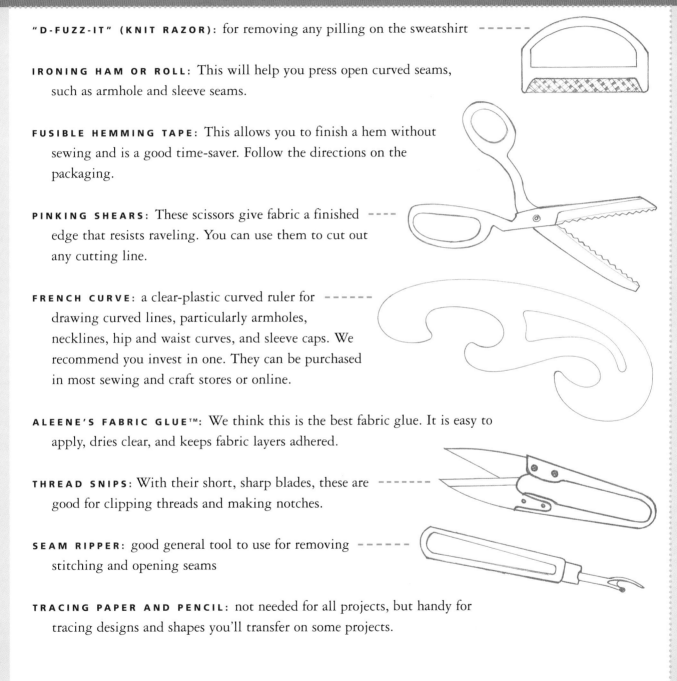

"D-FUZZ-IT" (KNIT RAZOR): for removing any pilling on the sweatshirt

IRONING HAM OR ROLL: This will help you press open curved seams, such as armhole and sleeve seams.

FUSIBLE HEMMING TAPE: This allows you to finish a hem without sewing and is a good time-saver. Follow the directions on the packaging.

PINKING SHEARS: These scissors give fabric a finished edge that resists raveling. You can use them to cut out any cutting line.

FRENCH CURVE: a clear-plastic curved ruler for drawing curved lines, particularly armholes, necklines, hip and waist curves, and sleeve caps. We recommend you invest in one. They can be purchased in most sewing and craft stores or online.

ALEENE'S FABRIC GLUE™: We think this is the best fabric glue. It is easy to apply, dries clear, and keeps fabric layers adhered.

THREAD SNIPS: With their short, sharp blades, these are good for clipping threads and making notches.

SEAM RIPPER: good general tool to use for removing stitching and opening seams

TRACING PAPER AND PENCIL: not needed for all projects, but handy for tracing designs and shapes you'll transfer on some projects.

Measuring Basics

Taking proper measurements is crucial for the perfect fit. We suggest having a friend take your measurements, as you will get more accurate results that way. It is critical to get your measurements right, in order to get the perfect fit in your reconstructed sweatshirt fashions.

Here are the body part measurements you need to take before starting your projects. You won't need every one of these measurements; each project uses some and not others.

Measure Up!

Always use a dressmaker's tape measure **when** measuring body parts, not a retractable metal one. Dressmaker's tape measures are made from cloth or plastic and are designed to lie flat as they wrap around curves and under and over body parts. They come in a variety of colors, and are available at sewing and craft stores or online.

For Shirts, Tops, and Jackets	For Sleeves	For Pants
Bust	Arm Length	Waist
High Bust	Wrist Circumference	Natural Hip
Waist	Armhole and	Lower Hip
Hip (needed only for	Sleeve Cap	Pant Length
hip-length and	Underarm Length	Thigh
longer tops)		Calf
Center Front Length	**For Skirts**	
Center Back Length	Waist	
Shoulder Width	Natural Hip	
Shoulder Length	Lower Hip	
Side Length	Skirt Length	
Full Length		

HOW TO TAKE BODY MEASUREMENTS

Measuring your body (bust, waist, hips, etc.) is the main component in determining the final body measurements you'll use in the projects. But there are two additional components you need to account for in your final body measurements—seam allowance and ease, or wearing ease. (You could not wear a garment that measured exactly the same as your body part measurements. A little extra room is required to allow you to walk, sit, and otherwise move in your clothes.

We use ½-inch seam allowances in our projects (unless otherwise specified). Ease is generally 2 inches total (1 inch ease in the front and 1 inch ease in the back).

Here's an easy-to-remember formula:

Body Part Measurement + Seam Allowance + Ease = Your Body Measurement

MEASURING FRONTS AND BACKS

In any overall body part measurement, the halves are rarely equal. For example, while overall your waist might measure 30 inches, the front waist could be 16½ inches and the back waist 13½ inches; a total bustline might measure 36 inches, with the front being 19 inches and the back 17 inches. Therefore, you need to measure the front and the back of your body separately when measuring the bust, waist, hips, etc.

TAKING MEASUREMENTS FOR SHIRTS, TOPS, JACKETS, SLEEVES, SKIRTS, AND PANTS

It is crucial that you keep your tape measure straight and level when measuring body parts.

It is best to take measurements wearing only undergarments, or fitted leggings and a tank top. Before you begin, you'll need to mark side seam lines on whatever you are wearing for the measurements (bra, panties, leggings, skin, etc.) using an erasable/washable pencil or marker. This side seam mark should be the halfway point between the front and back of the body, on the sides of the torso, waist, hips, and thighs (i.e., where the side seams of the shirts, pants, and skirts will fall). This way, you will be measuring from the same side seam point when you measure the front and the back of each body part.

Note: The ease measurements given below are for fitted garments. For looser-fitting garments, add more ease.

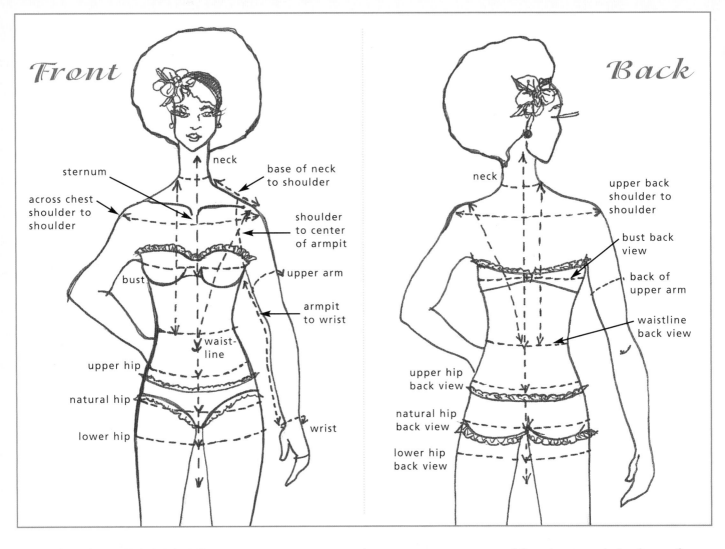

Front

- sternum
- neck
- base of neck to shoulder
- across chest shoulder to shoulder
- shoulder to center of armpit
- bust
- upper arm
- armpit to wrist
- waistline
- upper hip
- natural hip
- lower hip
- wrist

Back

- neck
- upper back shoulder to shoulder
- bust back view
- back of upper arm
- waistline back view
- upper hip back view
- natural hip back view
- lower hip back view

WHERE TO MEASURE: PERSONAL BODY MEASUREMENT CHART

MEASURING FULL LENGTH: Measure from the highest point of the shoulder, where it meets the neck, straight down over the bust to the waistline. Keep the tape measure parallel to your center front. _____

MEASURING UNDERARM LENGTH: Measure from 2 inches below armpit (about where the underarm of a sleeve would hit) down the inside of the arm to the wrist. _____

MEASURING NECK: Measure around the base of your neck, where the neck meets the shoulders. Measure front and back neck separately. Add 1-inch seam allowance and ½-inch ease to the front neck and also to the back neck.

FRONT NECK _____ BACK NECK _____

MEASURING FRONT BUST: (You must wear a bra when measuring front bust, unless you never wear a bra.) On front of body, measure across fullest part of bust from side seam to side seam. Add 1-inch seam allowance and 1-inch ease. _____

MEASURING FRONT HIGH BUST: Measure straight across front, about 3 inches up from the bust, from armhole to armhole. Add 1-inch seam allowance and 1-inch ease. _____

MEASURING BUSTLINE: Measure down the center of the front of your body, from the base of the neck to the level of the fullest part of the bust—the bustline (i.e., the nipple line). _____

MEASURING BUST POINT DISTANCE: Measure from nipple to nipple, straight across the bustline. Add ½-inch ease. _____

MEASURING FRONT WAIST: At your waist (about navel level), measure front of body from side seam to side seam. Add 1-inch seam allowance and 1-inch ease. _____

MEASURING FRONT HIP AND FRONT LOWER HIP.

FRONT HIP— At the side seam, measure 8–9 inches down from your waist to determine hip level. At this point, measure across front hipline from side seam to side seam. Add 1-inch seam allowance and 1-inch ease. _____

FRONT LOWER HIP: At the side seam, measure 11 inches down from your waist. At this point, measure across front lower hip from side seam to side seam. Add 1-inch seam allowance and 1-inch ease. _____

MEASURING CENTER FRONT LENGTH: Measure from the base of the neck, down the center front, to the waistline. _____

MEASURING FRONT SHOULDER WIDTH: Measure from the edge of the shoulder across the front upper chest to the same position at opposite side. Add 1 inch for ease. _____

MEASURING SHOULDER LENGTH: Measure the length of the shoulder from the neck to the end of the shoulder. _____

MEASURING ARM LENGTH: With your arm relaxed and hanging from your shoulder, measure along side of arm from top of shoulder, down to elbow, and then from elbow down to wrist bone. (Note: Let your arm hang down in a relaxed way. Do not lock your elbow when taking this measurement, keep it relaxed and bent.) Add 1-inch seam allowance and 1-inch ease. _____

MEASURING WRIST CIRCUMFERENCE: Wrap tape measure around wrist bone, then add 1-inch seam allowance and ease as desired. _____

MEASURING ARMHOLE CIRCUMFERENCE: This is a measurement you do not take on your body. The best way to accurately measure armhole circumference is to measure the armholes of the actual sweatshirt you are working on. Measure the front armhole and the back armhole separately. Lay the shirt flat on a tabletop, front side up, smoothing all wrinkles.

Measure the underarm seam, up around the curve of the armhole to the shoulder seam at the top of the armhole. Add 1-inch seam allowance. Repeat for back of armhole. _____

MEASURING SLEEVE CAPS: The sleeve cap is determined by the armhole circumference, plus ease. Sleeve cap ease is distributed across the entire top of the sleeve cap (there is no ease in the underarm portion of the sleeve). The amount of ease will vary depending on the style of the sleeve. A puffed sleeve requires a lot of extra ease (at least 4 inches), whereas an average, more fitted sleeve cap needs only 1 inch of ease. Be sure to add 1-inch seam allowance to the sleeve cap measurement. _____

MEASURING SKIRT LENGTH: Hold tape measure on side seam at your waistline, and let the tape measure hang free, dropping to floor. Note desired length (above, at, or below knee level). Add ½-inch seam allowance at waist, and hem measurement at bottom (2 inches for a traditional turned hem). Remember to wear whatever shoes you will wear with the garment when taking skirt length measurements. _____

MEASURING PANT LENGTH: Hold tape measure on the side at your waistline, and let the tape measure hang free, dropping to floor. Note desired length: above, below, or at knee; capri length; ankle length; or floor length. Add ½-inch seam allowance at waist, and hem measurement at bottom (2 inches for a traditional turned hem). Remember to wear whatever shoes you will wear with the garment when taking pant length measurements. _____

MEASURING THIGHS: Measure completely around your upper thigh at its widest point, being sure to keep tape measure flat and level. Add 1-inch seam allowance and ease as desired (1 inch for fitted thigh, more inches for looser fit). _____

Quick Tips for Taking Body Part Measurements

If you are taking your own measurements, stand in front of a full-length mirror to measure yourself. Use the mirror as your tool to help you place the tape measure in the correct position on each body part and to make sure the tape measure is straight and level as it wraps around your body.

If someone else is taking your measurements, stand directly in front of the person who is taking your measurements, at the same level.

Allow your arms to hang naturally. Do not raise your arms in the air or pull them away from your sides. Allow for a small space under your arms to slide the tape measure around the bust. Even when taking the bust measurement, your arms should hang naturally by your sides.

Stand in a relaxed position while maintaining an upright posture; do not slouch or bend or twist your body while taking measurements.

Do not pull the tape measure too tight or too loose. It should lie flat against the body and be completely level as it runs across your body. If it dips, it's too loose; if it rises up, it's too tight.

Do not hold your breath or suck in your stomach when measuring your waist. When measuring for skirt or pant length, allow the tape measure to hang freely to your desired length. Do not pull it taut.

When measuring for skirt or pant lengths, consider the heel height of the shoe or boot you'll wear with the garment. Wear that shoe or boot when taking these measurements. You can also measure the lengths of your own skirts and pants.

Marking

Y ou'll need just a few basic tools to mark the cutting and sewing lines for your projects. All these materials are available in sewing and craft shops or online.

Marking Tools

FABRIC MARKING PENS, PENCILS, OR TAILOR'S CHALK: The new air-soluble and wash-away pens and pencils are great to use because their pointed tips make accurate marks that are temporary, not permanent. Air-soluble markers disappear over time. Water-soluble markers can be washed away with water. Test all markers before using them, because some are permanently set by heat. Be sure to read the packaging of your purchased markers carefully to make sure they are temporary.

When selecting marking pencils or chalk, use white, yellow, or light blue, as these colors wash out or erase more easily than darker pencil colors. (You can use a regular No. 2 pencil for marking, but test it on your fabric first to make sure it erases or washes away easily.)

DRESSMAKER'S TRACING PAPER AND TRACING WHEEL: Stick to the white, yellow, and light blue colors. Red and black tracing papers do not iron out or wash out easily. (Do not use the black or dark blue paper carbon sheets used in office work.) Mark on both sides of the fabric simultaneously by placing a second sheet of tracing paper face up under the bottom layer. It helps to place a plastic mat or piece of cardboard underneath to keep the fabric from slipping as you roll the tracing wheel.

CLEAR RULERS: Clear plastic rulers are the best because you can see the seam lines, marking lines, and design details through them. You'll need just one ruler—an 18-by-2–inch drafting ruler is our top choice; a French curve is handy but optional.

puffier sleeve cap, the sleeve cap measurement should be longer than the armhole measurement.

FITTED SLEEVE CAP: For a fitted sleeve cap, the sleeve cap measurement minus the armhole measurement needs to be trimmed at the center top of the sleeve cap. For example: Let's say you need to lose 2 inches from the sleeve cap. At the center top of the sleeve cap, mark ½ inch to 1 inch in from the raw edge. Using a curved ruler (with curve at top), mark a new, shorter sleeve cap from this lower point, blending the new sleeve cap line into the existing underarm curve. Measure the sleeve cap. If the sleeve cap is still too long, lower the sleeve in ½-inch intervals until you get the measurement you want.

PUFFED OR GATHERED SLEEVE CAP: If you're starting with a large sleeve, you'll definitely have enough fabric in the sleeve cap to puff or gather the sleeve. Measure around the large sleeve cap, beginning at the outside edge and moving in from the edge in ½-inch increments, until you have the sleeve cap length you desire. A sleeve cap that is 1½-inches longer than the armhole will give you a gentle puff; add more inches for more dramatic puffs.

If your sweatshirt has fitted sleeves, you may need to make a new sleeve pattern and cut your sleeve out of a larger piece of sweat fabric. Sleeve cap ease is distributed across the top of the sleeve cap only, not across the underarm portion of the sleeve. Place a mark at each end of the sleeve cap—about 4 inches in from the underarm edge of the sleeve. Distribute the ease between the two points.

CREATING NEW SLEEVE PATTERNS: For some projects, you will create rather than adjust sleeves. Here is how to create a new sleeve pattern.

The easiest way is to use an existing sleeve pattern (like one from a sewing pattern) or an old shirtsleeve as a starting point. Following the instructions above for adjusting the sleeve cap, draw your new fitted (or puffy) cap directly on the pattern or the old sleeve. If you need to, tape extra paper or fabric to the top of the sleeve cap to accommodate a cap larger than the existing one.

Take this adjusted sleeve pattern and transfer it to your fabric. (See detailed illustrations for drawing a puffed sleeve cap on page 13.)

MARKING SLEEVE LENGTH: For a full-length sleeve, use your arm length measurement and measure straight down from the center of sleeve cap to wrist level (be sure to include extra for hem); mark and draw sleeve bottom line. Mark centerline at wrist level.

MARKING SKIRT AND PANT CUTTING LINES

Instructions for using your body measurements to mark skirts and pants will be found in specific project instructions. If you are having trouble taking accurate body measurements, you can measure a pair of pants or a skirt that fits you perfectly instead.

MARKING AND CUTTING NOTCHES

In many projects, you need to mark and cut notches. Notches are used to indicate beginning and ending stitching points, or matching points for two pieces that will be sewn together. For example, you'll mark and cut notches on the armholes and sleeve caps so that you can match them when stitching the sleeve cap into the armhole.

Mark the notch as directed. To cut the notch, using fabric or embroidery scissors, cut a small (⅛ to ¼ inch) slit at the notch mark.

Sewing Sweatshirt Fabric

Here are all the sewing techniques you'll need to make the projects in this book, whether you are sewing by hand or by machine. If you are a novice sewer, you can practice these stitches and techniques on scrap pieces of fabric before beginning a project.

BASTING AND GATHERING

Basting is a temporary stitch used to hold two fabric pieces together until they can be stitched together permanently. It is also used create gathers along a fabric edge. We recommend using brightly colored thread for this technique so that when you are finished it is easy to see which thread to remove.

Hand Basting

Using a handsewing needle and thread, take large running stitches (½- to 1 inch apart), about ¼ to ⅜ inch from the raw edge of the fabric, either through a single layer of fabric (for gathering) or two or more layers (for seams and other construction details).

Machine Basting

To baste a seam or other construction detail, use the longest machine stitch length available and machine baste fabric layers together inside the seam allowance (for example, with ½-inch seam allowance, machine baste ⅜ inches in from raw edges).

Gathering

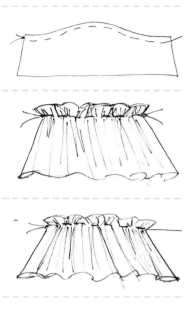

Gathering is a process of using long stitches to draw up a length of fabric into a shortened length, creating soft even folds that provide extra room or a design detail. You'll often find gathering in sleeve caps, under the bust, and at the bottoms of sleeves—anywhere you want to add fullness for either wearing ease or aesthetic appeal. You can gather along an entire seam line or part of one. Gathering is very easy to do, either by hand or by machine. Before you gather, mark the points at which the gathering should start and stop.

Hand Gathering

Hand baste through a single layer of fabric, about ¼ inch in from the raw edge. Pull threads from each end (like pulling a drawstring) until gathered piece is the desired length. Secure threads at ends by knotting them or wrapping around a pin. Adjust gathers, distributing them evenly between gathering points.

Machine Gathering

Some machines have a preset gathering stitch that stitches and gathers the fabric simultaneously. If your machine does not have automatic gathering capacity: Using the longest stitch length on your sewing machine, stitch between gathering points, ¼ inch in from raw edge. Pull the threads at each end (like a drawstring) until gathered piece is desired length. Secure thread ends as above. Adjust gathers, distributing them evenly between gathering points.

SEWING ELASTIC

We use elastic in our designs to cinch in waistlines and gather sleeve bottoms. Used this way, elastic allows for a comfortable fitted look that gives you room to move (and breathe). The elastic you use for these purposes will always be shorter than the fabric area where you will stitch it. For example, if you are placing elastic on a back waistline, you'd use 7 to 8 inches of elastic to gather an 8 to 10-inch section of fabric. We suggest you practice on scrap fabric before sewing elastic to your actual garment.

Sewing Elastic by Machine

STEP 1: Lay fabric piece flat with wrong side facing up; mark elastic placement lines on sweat fabric, as directed in project instructions. Lay elastic on sweat fabric, stretching elastic to fit. (The elastic is shorter than the length between marks on the sweat fabric.) Pin or hand baste elastic in place at one end of the elastic, if desired.

STEP 2: Place all layers under presser foot and, using a small stitch length (10–12 stitches per inch), stitch elastic to fabric piece along each long edge of elastic (when sewing elastic to waist) or down center of elastic (for sleeves), stretching elastic as you stitch. Backstitch at the beginning and end of stitching.

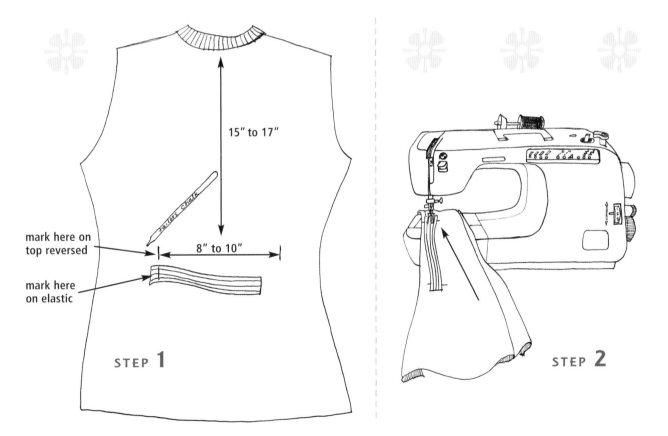

15" to 17"

mark here on top reversed

8" to 10"

mark here on elastic

STEP **1**

STEP **2**

FINISHES FOR EDGES, SEAMS, AND HEMS

There is minimal fraying on the raw edges of sweat fabrics, but they tend to roll a bit, especially if cut on the bias. We like to use the following edge and hem finishes to both prevent fraying and keep the edges lying flat.

Machine Finishes for Seams or Edges

- Zigzag Stitch with Regular Sewing Machine
- Zigzag stitch ¼ inch from raw edges of cut pieces or from raw edges of stitched seam allowances

Serger or Overlock Machines

If you have a serger or overlock machine, serge raw edges of cut pieces or raw edges of stitched seam allowances.

Finished Hems

You don't have to finish all the hemlines on our projects, but when you do, remember to add the hem allowance to your finished length.

SIMPLE HEM: Fold fabric edge over ⅜ inch toward wrong side, then fold again ½ inch. From wrong side, topstitch (see page 19) ⅛ inch from folded edge, through all thicknesses. If sewing by hand, whipstitch (see page 20) folded edge to wrong side.

TUNNEL HEM: On some projects, we finish the hems of pants, skirts, blouses, and sleeves with a drawstring. The channel, or tunnel the drawstring runs through, forms a tunnel hem. To make it, fold the hem width (diameter of drawstring, plus ½-inch ease) to the wrong side; pin. From the wrong side, sew with a straight stitch ⅛ to ¼ inch from raw edge, leaving an opening through which to insert and pull through the drawstring.

NO-SEW HEMS: Spread a thin layer of fabric glue on the wrong side of the hem, close to the raw edge. Fold hem to wrong side along hemline, pressing raw edge with fingers so hem adheres to wrong side of fabric. Allow glue to dry before wearing. You can topstitch close to the folded hem once the glue has dried, if desired.

FUSIBLE HEMMING TAPE: Cut a piece of iron-on hemming tape the same length as the hemline. Fold hem along hemline toward wrong side of garment. Sandwich hemming tape between wrong side of hem and wrong side of garment, about ⅛ to ¼ inch from raw edge of hem. Fuse layers together using a hot, dry iron.

SEAM ALLOWANCES

Seam allowances are always ½ inch, unless otherwise specified.

SNAPS

STEP 1: Place snap part with the ball over snap placement marking.

STEP 2: Sew several small stitches close together through each hole of snap, picking up threads from the garment with each stitch. Carry thread under the snap from hole to hole.

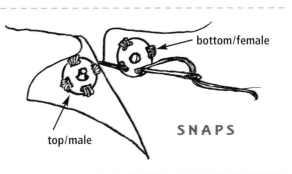

bottom/female

top/male

SNAPS

TOPSTITCHING

We use topstitching on many of our designs because it emphasizes the structural lines of garments and, when applied to seams, keeps them flat and crisp. Topstitching can be done by hand or by machine.

TOPSTITCHING BY MACHINE: Use buttonhole thread in the needle, all-purpose thread in the bobbin, and a stitch length of 6 to 8 stitches per inch. Test on scrap fabric before sewing in case you need to adjust the tension. Stitch on garment where directed, slowing down at curves and pivoting at corners. You can stitch two lines of topstitching, ⅛ to ¼ inch apart, if you desire. Leave thread tails long so they can be worked to the wrong side of the fabric with a handsewing needle.

TOPSTITCHING BY HAND: Use buttonhole thread and a long sewing needle. Anchor thread on wrong side, and make even-length (about ⅛ to ¼ inch), evenly spaced stitches (about ⅛ to ¼ inch), going in and out of the fabric.

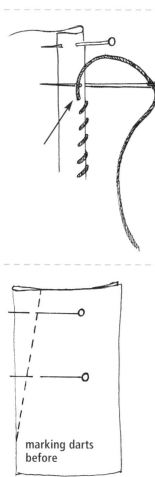

marking darts
before

folding darts
after

WHIPSTITCH

A whipstitch is a hand stitch used to finish edges or to attach one piece of fabric to another.

WHIPSTITCH AN EDGE: Insert needle perpendicular to the edge, from the wrong side through to the right side of the fabric, about ⅛ to ¼ inch from edge. Keep stitches evenly spaced.

WAIST DARTS ON BOTTOMS

Waist darts take up excess fabric at the waistline, so the garment fits smoothly across the belly, the hips, and over the backside.

On both the back and the front, determine the excess amount of fabric at the waistline, and divide that measurement in half. This will be the width of each dart. For example, 2 inches of excess fabric equals two 1-inch darts.

MARKING DARTS: Make all marks on wrong side of fabric. Make a mark 3 ½ inches on either side of center back (or center front) waist; mark. This is the center of your dart. Draw a line straight down from this mark about 3 to 3 ½ inches; mark—this is the end of your dart. Mark out half the dart width on each side of the centerline. For 1-inch dart, mark out ½ inch on each side of centerline. Draw slanted lines from these marks to bottom of dart mark.

SEWING DARTS (BY HAND OR MACHINE): Fold each dart along centerline of dart, matching slanted lines. Stitch dart, by hand or by machine, along slanted lines. Do not backstitch at end of dart. Leave enough thread length to tie knots to secure darts.

BUTTONS AND BUTTONHOLES

Mark button placements and buttonhole placement lines on right side of garment, as directed in projects.

MARK BUTTONHOLE (HORIZONTAL OR VERTICAL): Begin marking for buttonhole(s) ⅛ inch on either side of the buttonhole placement line. (This allows for the fact that the button will "pull" away from the closing when garment is worn.) The length of your buttonhole should be equal to the diameter of your button.

STITCH BUTTONHOLE: Use the buttonhole foot and buttonhole stitch selection of your choice on your sewing machine. Or mark your buttonholes and have your local dry cleaner or dressmaker/tailor service sew them for you. If you are sewing by hand, you can make a series of very closely spaced whipstitches (see page 20) all around the buttonhole mark, leaving room for a slit in the center of stitching. Once buttonhole is stitched, cut/slit fabric inside buttonhole stitching.

GLUING BASICS

You can use fabric glue instead of pins to secure seams before stitching or to adhere embellishments to the garment before stitching them on. We recommend using Aleene's Fabric Glue because it isn't stiff and doesn't wash away with repeated laundering. Here are some basic rules about using glue:

1. Work on a flat, even surface when gluing.

2. Your fabric surface should be clean and free of any debris.

3. Never use too much glue. It is best to spread a thin layer of glue on both surfaces to be bonded. Do it in the same manner as buttering toast. We suggest using some sort of spreading tool, such as a Popsicle stick, a wooden coffee stirrer, or a strip of cardboard about ½ inch wide and 4 or 5 inches long, cut from an old shoe box.

4. Allow the glue to get tacky. In other words, after applying a thin layer of glue to both surfaces, wait 30 seconds before placing the fabrics together.

5. Once your two fabric surfaces are glued together, put something heavy on top of the piece: books, or sewing weights if you have them. Leave it like this for about 20 to 30 minutes, for secure glue bonding. You may want to sandwich a layer of cardboard or wax paper between the books and the glued piece, just in case there is any leakage.

6. Always place a piece of cardboard, paper, or wax paper between the back and front layers of fabric when gluing something to just the front or top layer of fabric. Otherwise, the glue can seep through and bond layers you don't want glued together. Likewise, place cardboard or paper between the garment you are gluing and the work surface, to prevent the glue from leaking through and adhering your garment to the surface.

7. Allow glue to dry before stitching over it, or the wet glue will clog your sewing machine or handsewing needle.

8 QUICK TIPS FOR SEWING SWEATS

TIP 1: Always be sure to read, read, and read again. Make sure to take a moment to clearly understand the step-by-step instructions for each project before you begin. It will save you a lot of time and mistakes.

TIP 2: No matter what level of sewing experience you have, always test difficult techniques on a scrap piece of fabric before starting your project.

TIP 3: Due to the heavy weight of sweatshirt fabric, it is crucial to have the proper handsewing and/or machine (if you are using one) needles. Your handsewing needles should include an assortment of embroidery, darning, and all-purpose needles. Your sewing machine needles should vary from 12, 14, 16, and 18 points, depending on the project. Make sure to use sharp fabric scissors.

TIP 4: Be sure to have a variety of contrasting colored thread. This is great for decorative details and also helps you to see your basting stitches, making them easy to remove after your garment is completed. We suggest using high-quality thread that will not snap easily.

TIP 5: Use quilting straight pins; they are larger and can hold bulky materials together, yet they are thin enough to run through a sewing machine without breaking your needles.

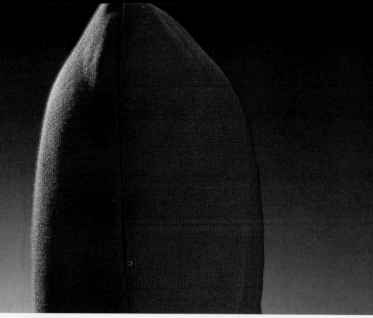

TIP 6: Practice the stitching techniques that will be used throughout the projects. Because sweatshirt fabric has some stretch to it, you'll want to stitch around raw edges to keep them from stretching out of shape as you work. The most commonly used hand stitches are whipstitch, blanket stitch, and cross stitch; and by sewing machine, the zigzag stitch. For those of you who are experienced sewing divas and have access to a serger or overlock machine, you'll find it is your best friend on these projects.

TIP 7: When gluing appliqués or other embellishments, be very careful not to apply too much adhesive. The sweat fabric absorbs liquid very quickly and the glue may bleed through to the other side of your garment, which will cause certain fabrics to get nappy and hard.

TIP 8: Remember to have fun with these projects. Always keep a recycler's mind-set: Mistakes can be turned into lovely appliqués or other accessories like belts, a waist sash, or even a strap on a handbag. Plus, recycling your threads is one small step to being more eco-friendly.

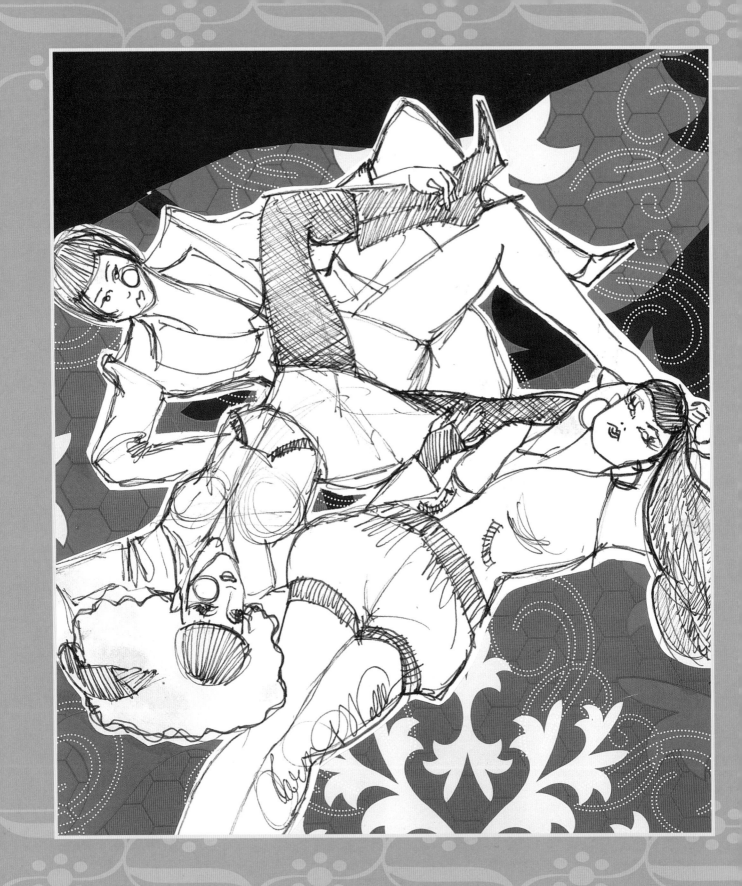

Selecting Sweatshirts

How to choose makeover sweat styles that play up your best features (and play down what you want to minimize)

When choosing sweatshirts, pants, or hoodies to wear unaltered, we suggest you NOT go for oversize fits. While large (i.e., too big) might be comfortable, it is the most unflattering look on any type of figure. It gives you a frumpy, "I am trying to hide my figure" look.

When choosing sweats for your projects, however, we advise the opposite. For these recycled styles, the larger the sweats, the better. The sweats are your blank canvas, and the more sweat fabric you have to work with, the more design options you will have. Therefore, we suggest you use sweats sized medium, large, extra large, and extra extra large for these projects. Vintage, secondhand, and thrift sweats will bring novelty and character to the look. Major fashion labels send their fabrics out to specialty manufacturers to distress them for this worn, aged look, so look for older sweatshirts—they are prime candidates for refashioning.

Fun Facts About Sweats

The word **"sweatshirt"** entered the American lexicon in the **1920s**.

Once upon a time, sweats were considered apparel for only the athletic. The **first** sweatshirts were **utilitarian gray**, used exclusively as **athletic gear**, worn before and after games to keep the body warm.

Sweats take in perspiration, since most are made from **absorbent stretch cotton**. They keep the body warm during highly physical activity, therefore preventing athletic injuries; hence, the origin of one of many sweat nicknames—**the warm-up**.

In 1919, **Abe and Bill Feinbloom**, founders of the Knickerbocker Knitting Company and Champion Athletic Wear, owned a mill that produced sweaters. In the 1930s, the Feinbloom brothers patented a flocking process to place raised letters on clothing—and they began to produce athletic clothing. The '60s hit, and the sporting of university names and logos on sweatshirts became the thing to do. The Feinbloom brothers also created the sideline sweatshirt, known in contemporary fashion lingo as **the zip-front hoodie**. The sideline sweat was designed for the football player market, because the zip front made it easier for players to get in and out of their sweats during games. Teams across the world embraced the practicality of **the zip-front sweatshirt.**

The jogging or **track suit**, a sweat suit of matching pants and jacket, became popular. Initally worn for jogging in the 1970s, the tracksuit evolved into style-conscious apparel. In the late 1970s, designer **Norma Kamali** was one of the first designers to use sweatshirt material for women's fashion jackets, skirts, and pants.

The '80s were booming with wild fashion. The beginning of the hip-hop era was in full swing. Polyester Adidas tracksuits were an all-time favorite, making it easier for B-boys to break-dance on hardwood floors. It was also a fashion statement to rock the tracksuit even when not dancing! Juicy Couture took sexiness up a notch with formfitting velour jogging suits. Looking frumpy in a sweatshirt is a thing of the past. **Sweats have come a long way, baby.**

Sweats are still used for old-school purposes such as working out and casual activity, but the transformation of the once-utilitarian gray sweatshirt into the **glamorous style staple** in your wardrobe deserves recognition.

Body Basics

It does not matter how good a garment looks if it does not fit the body. The goal of dressing is to emphasize the positive points of your body. This is a learning process. No matter your shape or size, you can always find clothing complementary to your body type. There are several body camouflaging techniques that will spotlight the positive elements of your body. Adopt these techniques to maximize every opportunity for a more vibrant, well-fitted wardrobe.

The best silhouette is one of ultimate balance. The goal of flattering dressing is to create the foolproof vertical line. When your eyes skim from head to toe without interruptions, your body looks longer and thinner.

On the next two pages you'll see a few do's and don'ts to lock into your memory bank.

DON'T: CUT THE BODY IN HALF WITH CONTRASTING COLORS.

DON'T: CREATE HORIZONTAL LINES WITH UNFLATTERING PATTERNS.

DON'T: WEAR OVERSIZE CLOTHING IN HOPES OF DISGUISING BODY FLAWS.

DON'T: WEAR CLOTHING THAT IS TOO TIGHT.

-chic sweats

DOs & DON'Ts

DON'T ● ●

Cut the body in half with contrasting colors.

> Unless your proportions are absolutely perfect, cutting your body in half is a fashion no-no. Slicing your body in half can be jarring.

Wear clothing that is too tight.

> Slim or voluptuous, too-tight clothing is unattractive.

Wear oversize clothing in hopes of disguising body flaws. You'll just look like you're wearing clothes that are too big.

Create horizontal lines with unflattering patterns, especially across the largest part of your body.

DO ● ●

Cut the body in thirds; it is more pleasing to the eye.

> Wear longer slacks or dresses with cropped tops.

> Wear longer cardigans or tunics with shorter skirts.

> This helps to create less jarring lines.

Aim to elongate your vertical line.

DO: WEAR LONGER SLACKS OR DRESSES WITH CROPPED TOPS. WEAR LONGER CARDIGANS OR TUNICS WITH SHORTER SKIRTS.

DO: AIM TO ELONGATE YOUR VERTICAL LINE.

Camouflaging Figure Flaws

TOP-HEAVY: You tend to carry weight in the midriff, and your shoulders are broader than your hips. You want to balance out the lower half of your body. Refrain from using details on tops such as sequins and patch pockets, especially across the chest and shoulders. V-necks are a must for you because they distract from your shoulders and focus attention on the center of your upper body, creating the ultimate vertical line.

BOTTOM-HEAVY: You tend to carry most of your weight in your hips and derriere, and your shoulders and waist are much smaller than your hips. Your goal is to minimize the hips and increase the width of the shoulders. Add shoulder details such as epaulets and small shoulder pads (be careful with shoulder pads or you'll end up looking like an NFL player). Wear flowing skirts and loose slacks. Wide-leg pants, in particular, are your friends. Lose details on the derriere. Wear horizontal details across the front to increase the width of your shoulders.

RECTANGULAR: Your body lacks a waistline, so your primary goal is to create one. Wear shirts that cinch at the waist or gather in the back; slight drawstring gathering gives the hint of a waistline indentation. Straight-leg pants with tunics are great for rectangular bodies because they create a more feminine body line by de-emphasizing your lack of a waistline. Avoid stiff or boxy shapes, as they mirror your body's overall square characteristics. Embrace styles with gentle curves to counterbalance your columnar silhouette.

ROUND: Your body type is full-figured. Your goal is to create a leaner, longer silhouette. Stay away from clingy fabrics that stick too tightly to your frame. Wear fluid fabrics that skim the natural outline of your body. Blouson-style tops look great on you because they move freely and don't cling to problem areas. Sport wide-leg trousers or jeans, which are not only in vogue but also de-emphasize full hips and a belly. A-line skirts camouflage wide hips and define the waist, as do wrap dresses. Both are fabulous on a round body type.

SHORT WAIST: Your legs tend to be long in proportion to the rest of your body. Your challenge is to lengthen your upper torso. Create vertical and strong diagonal lines above the waist. Look to elongate the torso with deep V-necks and bold accessories such as scarves and long necklaces. Wear tops that fall below the belt line; they make your waist look lower than it is. Wear belts the same color as your top so you don't break your upper body into two parts.

LONG WAIST: Your legs are shorter in proportion to the rest of your body, making the waist look long. Your aim is to make your legs appear longer. Empire waists work well for you because they help shorten the torso. Wide belts also help raise the waist, especially when the belt color matches your bottom, which helps create the illusion of longer legs. Avoid pedal pushers, capris, and hip-huggers—they make your legs look shorter.

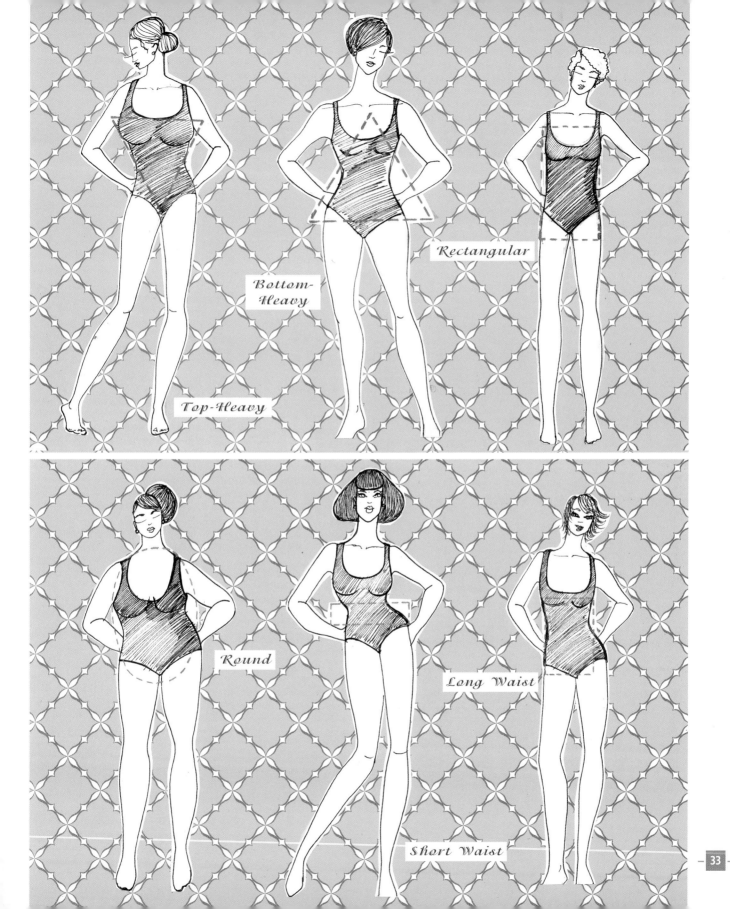

Top-Heavy

Bottom-Heavy

Rectangular

Round

Long Waist

Short Waist

Monochromatic Dressing

This is one of the easiest ways to camouflage undesired body imbalances. If you're color junkies like us (we, at times, overdose on color!), this may sound boring. Don't fret; there are infinite shades of a single color that can be used in a monochromatic ensemble. When wearing a single color from top to bottom, you create the desired vertical line. To slenderize, mix up the spectrum of a single color in your monochromatic look.

Mixing Monochromatic Textures

Play with texture in the same color family. A navy cord blazer on top of an oxford-blue button-front shirt over a blue wool plaid skirt is flattering. The assortment of textures increases the dimension, giving your monochromatic ensemble a fuller look.

Of course, you can break the monochromatic rule with a hint of color. Do this with accessories. Vibrant red shoes or turquoise drop earrings add a splash of color to a monochromatic ensemble.

NECKLINES

Your neck is the best-kept secret when it comes to choosing styles that flatter your body. When you elongate your neck, you automatically look taller. Necklines frame the face, which is the nucleus of your body structure. Your face, the home of your eyes, is the gateway to your soul. Wear necklines that balance the shape of your face.

The Perfect Bra

The right bra does the body good. It can lift, minimize, or enlarge, depending on your bra-ly needs.

Universal Necklines

The most universal neckline is the V-neck. Most face shapes can wear Vs. The V-neckline can make a small chest more interesting or minimize a large bust. It can minimize shoulder width by creating vertical lines above the waist.

A General Rule about Necklines

Opposites attract! When choosing necklines, wear the opposite of your face shape. It's all about equal proportions. The contrast brings balance and highlights your communication center point!

Determining
the Shape of Your Face

Is it heart-shaped, square, round, rectangular, oval, triangular, or diamond shaped? Here are some tips about how to use the shape of your face to create the most flattering necklines for you.

HEART:
Narrow at jawline and chin, wide at temples and hairline. Heart-shaped faces can wear all necklines. Because your cheekbones are two of the wider points on your face, the most flattering neckline is the V-neck. You'll also look great in scoops, square necks, and crew necks.

ROUND:
Your face is as wide as it is long. Vs and squares are particularly complementary, since they contrast the shape of you face. If you're feeling glamorous, off-the-shoulder is also a winner. Avoid crew necks, since they crowd round faces by shortening the neck, which shrinks the entire body—a fashion no-no.

RECTANGULAR OR OBLONG:
Long and slender face, about the same width at forehead and just below cheekbones, with a narrow chin and/or very high forehead. Wear scoop necks! Since your face is square, the contrasting neckline is becoming. Avoid square necks; they further emphasize your strong jawline.

OVAL:
Slightly narrower at the jawline than at the temples, with a gently rounded hairline. This is the most proportional face shape. You can wear every neckline. Enjoy the gamut of possibilities!

TRIANGULAR:
Reverse of the heart shape—a dominant jawline with narrowing at the cheekbone and temples. You can wear all necklines; this face type can handle the versatility.

SQUARE:

Forehead, cheekbones, and jawline all the about the same width; squared jaw most prominent feature. Wear scoops. Avoid square necklines—they emphasize the most prominent feature on your face. Vs are also fantastic for this face type.

DIAMOND:

Widest at cheekbones; narrow forehead and jawline of approximately equal widths. Wear all necklines. Go crazy.

SHORT-NECKED:

Avoid excessive material around the neck. Cowls, crews, turtlenecks, and mandarin collars have the tendency to further shrink your neck. Wear V-necks or scoops to expose more of your neckline.

LONG-NECKED:

Please do not complain! You can wear every neckline, as you have the real estate to do so. Enjoy the versatility!

Styling Fashion Sweats to Enhance Your Body

When transforming your sweats into couture apparel, think about the strengths and weaknesses of your body. If you want to decrease the width of your shoulders, avoid putting details on them. If you want to lengthen your torso, lengthen your shirt to hit below your belt buckle.

All of the rules can be broken, depending upon your dressing needs and personal style. Play around with the wardrobe in your closet. Get to know your body. Experiment with different ensembles as you learn what clothing looks best on you. The objective is to ALWAYS dress in clothing that makes you look stellar.

sweat
PROJECTS

HERE ARE 22 EXCITING, CUTTING-EDGE FASHION
STATEMENTS FOR YOU TO MAKE OUT OF THE 'LOWLY'
SWEATSHIRT, HOODIE, AND PANT. BUT, BEFORE YOU
START, PLEASE TAKE NOTE OF THE FOLLOWING:

Before You Start

Skill Levels

We have rated the skill level for each project from 1 to 4, with level 1 being the easiest and level 4 the most difficult. But even if you are a novice sewer, feel free to tackle more difficult projects. You'll be surprised at what you can accomplish.

LEVEL 1 • •
Very easy; little to no sewing skills required

LEVEL 2 • •
Easy; beginner sewing skills a plus but not required

LEVEL 3 • •
Intermediate; advanced beginner sewing skills

LEVEL 4 • •
Advanced; intermediate sewing skills

General Notes

Depending on your body shape and size, you may have to adjust particular given measurements as needed.

Cutting lines in the step-by-step illustrations are always represented by a dashed line. Solid lines indicate measurements and should not be cut. Page references to how-to instructions for specific stitches and techniques are cited throughout project instructions. Definitions of terms can be found in the Glossary.

You can substitute fabric colors and embellishments, and adjust sleeve and hem lengths to personalize any design.

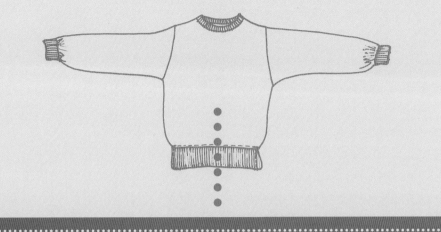

Hoodies

Hoodies are in full swing. We see hooded sweatshirts at least once a day, worn by diverse groups in various settings. This section is dedicated to ensuring that yours stands out from all the rest.

sleeveless cinched-waist hoodie

SKILL LEVEL: 2

REQUIRED TIME:

BY MACHINE:

  40 MINUTES

BY HAND:

  1 ½ HOURS

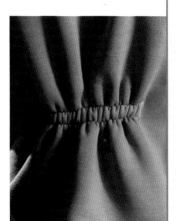

N o one will mistake you for one of the guys in this hoodie! This is the hoodie for the twenty-first century—flirty, hip, and a great layering piece for any season. It's sleeveless, so wear it alone or over a cute T-shirt of any sleeve length or style, with the bottom of your choice. The cinched-back waist is figure-flattering for all body types, and the contrasting topstitching directs visual interest up to the face.

Materials

STANDARD MATERIALS

Fabric scissors

Marking devices

Measuring devices

Quilting straight pins (or other heavy-duty straight pins)

Thread in matching or contrasting color

Iron and ironing board

Sewing machine and sewing machine needles (optional) Handsewing
   needles

SPECIAL MATERIALS

One zip-front hoodie, one size *larger* than you normally wear
   1-inch-wide elastic, 7 inches

zip-front hoodie with puff sleeves

SKILL LEVEL: 2

REQUIRED TIME:

BY MACHINE:

1 HOUR

BY HAND:

1½ HOURS

T he signature Sistahs of Harlem puff sleeve is always on the move. It settled down here, in another fantastic layering piece. This short puff looks stunning on top of long-sleeve shirts and can be worn with every style of bottom.

When layering it on top of short sleeves, make sure the shirt's sleeves are shorter than the hoodie's sleeves, or you'll have people asking you "What's that fabric hanging from under the sleeve?" If your arms are short, do not layer this over three-quarter-length sleeves. It will cut your arms in half, making them look even shorter.

Materials

STANDARD MATERIALS

Fabric scissors

Marking devices

Measuring devices

Quilting straight pins (or other heavy-duty straight pins)

Thread in matching or contrasting color

Iron and ironing board

Sewing machine and sewing machine needles (optional)

Handsewing needles

SPECIAL MATERIALS

One zip-front hoodie, one size *larger* than you normally wear

1-inch-wide elastic, 7 inches

¼-inch-wide elastic, 16 to 20 inches

6. Machine stitch elastic to hoodie (see page 17). Turn hoodie right side out.

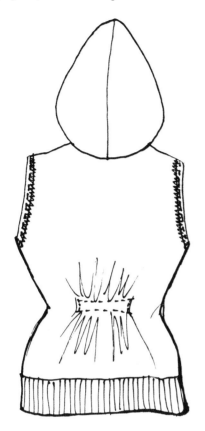

7. Using sleeves cut off in Step 1, lay sleeves flat, with right sides out, stacked one on top of the other. Mark cutting line ¼ inch inside sleeve seam from armhole to cuff (A). Cut through all layers of both sleeves, following cutting line. (You can mark and cut sleeves one at a time, if you prefer.) Open sleeves and lay flat, with wrong sides facing in, on top of each other (B).

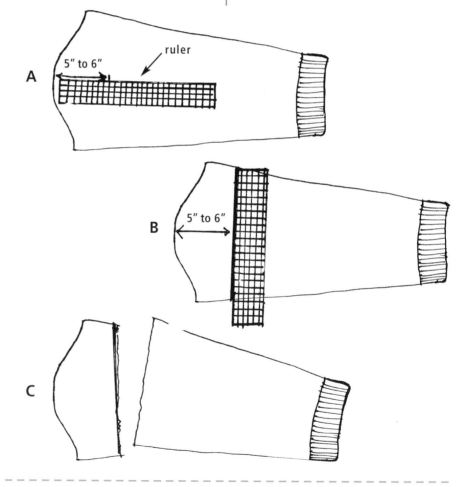

8. Beginning at center top of sleeve (i.e., top of sleeve cap), use ruler and measure down center of each sleeve 5 to 6 inches, depending on sleeve length desired; mark (A). (If you prefer more volume in the puff, measure down 7 to 8 inches.)

Place ruler horizontally across sleeve just below mark, and mark straight line across sleeve from edge to edge (B).

Cut across both sleeves following cutting line (C). Put bottoms of sleeves aside.

9. Keep sleeve tops cut in Step 8 flat and on top of each other. Using scissors, cut small notch at center top of sleeves. (This will help you match sleeve to hoodie shoulder seam in Step 11.)

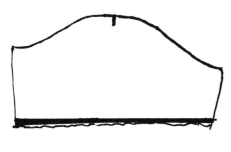

10. Separate your sleeves. Machine or hand baste across top of each sleeve $\frac{1}{2}$ inch from curved edge (see pages 15 and 16).

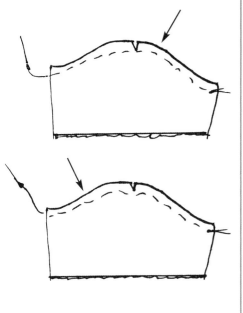

11. Pull basting thread in a drawstring manner to gather top of each sleeve (see page 16).

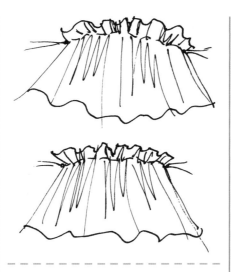

12. With wrong sides of sleeves facing right sides of hoodie, pin one gathered sleeve into each armhole of hoodie, matching center notch on sleeve to shoulder seam of hoodie. Topstitch (see page 19) sleeves to armholes through both fabric layers. NOTE: Sleeve cap extends only halfway down armhole.

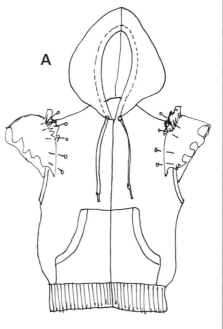

A

B

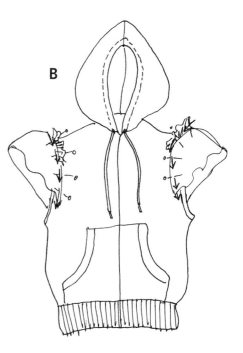

13. Cut $\frac{1}{4}$-inch-wide elastic equal to half bottom sleeve edge length. Place elastic on wrong side of sleeve, about $\frac{1}{2}$ inch from bottom raw edge. Machine or hand stitch elastic to sleeve (see page 17).

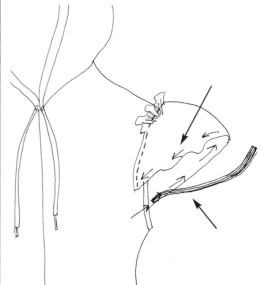

hoodie with bishop sleeves

SKILL LEVEL: 4

REQUIRED TIME:

BY MACHINE:

2 HOURS

BY HAND:

3½ HOURS

J azz up an ordinary outfit with our arresting bishop-sleeve hoodie. This style is for the bold woman whose everyday casual is never simple. The vintage royal-blue sweatshirt fabric sets off the dramatic bishop sleeves made of red-and-black graphic tees. (We suggest choosing contrasting sleeve colors for the extra punch.)

Don't limit yourself to tees for your sleeves; they can also be made from vintage sweaters or men's dress shirts, or if you're aiming for ultraglam, try suede or silk. For the drawstring detail on the sleeve, it's your choice. We suggest ribbon, cording, lace, or sweatshirt scraps.

Materials

STANDARD MATERIALS

Fabric scissors

Marking devices

Measuring devices

Quilting straight pins (or other heavy-duty straight pins)

Thread in matching or contrasting color

Iron and ironing board

Sewing machine and sewing machine needles (optional)

Handsewing needles

SPECIAL MATERIALS

One hoodie sweatshirt, your size

One graphic T-shirt, size XL

Two coordinating T-shirts, size XL

1-inch-wide elastic, 7 inches

1 yard ribbon or cording for sleeve drawstrings, optional

1. Using iron, press hoodie and T-shirts. Put T-shirts aside. Lay hoodie flat, right side out, and fold in half along center front, matching shoulder and armhole seams. Using measuring and marking devices, mark cutting line along sleeve/armhole seam line, as shown. Using fabric scissors, cut sleeves off along cutting line, through all layers of fabric. Put hoodie sleeves aside. You will use them in Step 14.

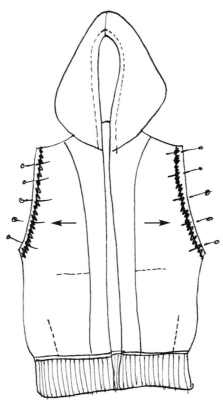

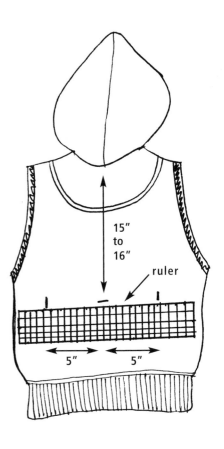

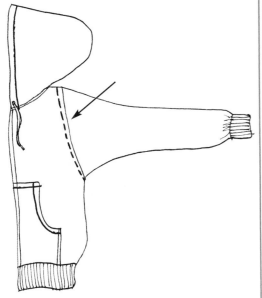

2. Turn hoodie wrong side out and lay flat with front facing up. Fold ¼-inch hem around each armhole and pin. Topstitch hem (see page 19) close to raw edge. If topstitching by hand, use short stitches, spaced close together.

3. Keep hoodie wrong side out and lay flat with back facing up. Beginning at neckline, measure down center back of hoodie to waist level (about 15 to 16 inches). Mark. (You can also measure above or below waist level, depending on where you want the cinched waist to fall. We prefer the exact waist.) Center ruler, horizontally, under mark. Measure out 5 inches in each direction from mark. Mark these points.

4. (A) Cut 7-inch length of 1-inch-wide elastic. Mark elastic at center and 1 inch in from each raw edge. Keep hoodie wrong side out with back facing up. Place elastic horizontally along waist, under marks, matching center of elastic to center mark on hoodie and side markings of elastic to corresponding side marks on hoodie (B). Pin in place.

5. Machine stitch elastic to hoodie (C) (see page 17).

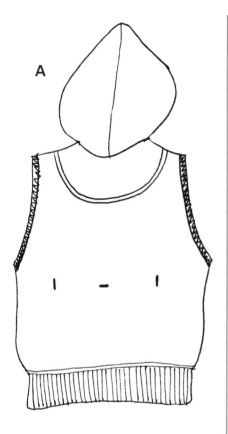

A

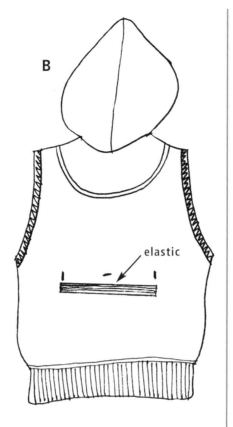

B

elastic

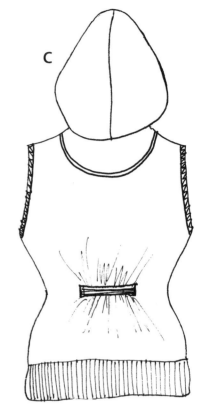

C

Bishop Sleeves

6. Lay graphic T-shirt flat, right side out, front facing up (A). Fold T-shirt in half along center front, matching shoulder and armhole seams. Pin together. Mark cutting lines down side seam, just above bottom hem (bottom of sleeve), and another, curved cutting line (for sleeve cap), equal to half armhole measurement, beginning at center front neckline and ending 1 inch below underarm (top of sleeve), as shown. See page 14 for marking sleeve cap cutting lines. Cut along all cutting

lines through all fabric layers. You now have two center sleeve pieces.

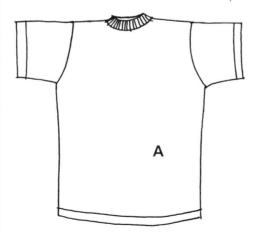

A

Put A pieces, cutoff hem, and sleeve to the side; you will use them later.

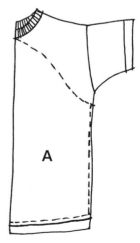

A

7. Lay one coordinating T-shirt flat, right side out, front facing up, and fold in half along center front, matching shoulder and armhole seams (B). Mark cutting line across T-shirt at armhole level. Mark another cutting line down center front, and another along side seam. Cut along all cutting lines through all fabric layers. Repeat on other coordinating T-shirt. You now have four rectangular pieces (B).

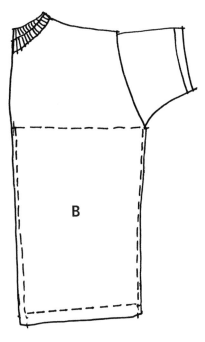

8. Take one A piece (still folded along center front), and two B pieces, and lay flat, next to each other, as shown. On B pieces, mark diagonal cutting line from upper left corner to lower right corner, beginning 1 inch to right of upper left corner, as shown. Cut along cutting lines. Repeat for remaining A and B pieces. Trim pieces along lower edges, if necessary, so they are the same length.

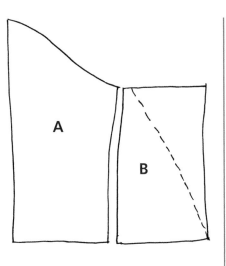

9. Use two A sleeve pieces and four B sleeve pieces to assemble the sleeves. Lay one A sleeve piece flat and right side up. With right sides facing, place straight cut edge of one B piece along one edge of A piece and pin, as shown. Repeat on opposite side of A piece. Stitch seams in direction indicated by arrows. Press seams flat.

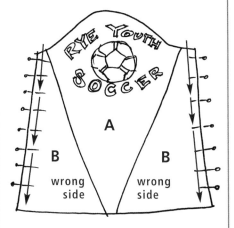

10. Open both sleeves and lay flat, right side up. Mark center of each sleeve at top of sleeve curve. Cut notches at marks.

11. Fold each sleeve in half lengthwise, with right sides facing. Pin and then stitch seam in direction indicated by arrows, stopping 2 inches above bottom edge of sleeve. Repeat for other sleeve.

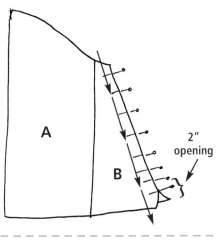

12. Turn hoodie wrong side out and lay flat, with back side facing up. Insert sleeve into armhole with right sides facing; pin sleeve to armhole, matching notch at center top of sleeve to hoodie shoulder seam, and underarm seam of sleeve to underarm seam of hoodie. NOTE: Sleeve will be inside hoodie, as shown by dotted line in illustration. Stitch each sleeve to hoodie in direction indicated by arrows.

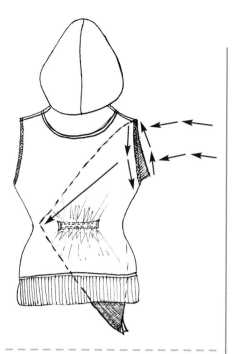

14. To make casing at bottom of sleeves for drawstrings, lay hoodie flat, right side out, with front facing up. Fold 1¼ inch at bottom of sleeves to wrong side and pin. NOTE: Pins are placed on right side, not wrong side, of sleeves. From right side, stitch around sleeve hems 1 inch from folded edge of sleeve bottoms in direction indicated by arrows.

NOTE: Since seam of sleeve stops 2 inches from hem, each end of sleeve hem casing will be open.

Take drawstrings made above. Using large safety pin in one end of drawstring, thread drawstring through one open end of casing, pulling with safety pin until drawstring comes out other end of casing. Repeat for other sleeve.

15. Pull drawstring ends, gathering sleeves at hems, and tie into bows, as shown. Then tie knot at end of each drawstring end to prevent drawstring from slipping out of casing.

NOTE: Gather sleeve hems to size that fits wrist, while allowing hand to pass through.

13. Making sleeve drawstrings:

Option 1: Use hoodie sleeves. Mark cutting line at top folded edge of each sleeve 1 inch from folded edge and just above sleeve cuff. Cut along cutting lines. You have two strips, each 2 inches wide and the length of sleeves, minus cuffs.

Option 2: Use leftover T-shirt scraps cut into 2-inch strips. NOTE: You may need to stitch strips together at 2-inch edges to create longer strips. Make two strips, each at least 18 inches long.

casing openings for draw-strings

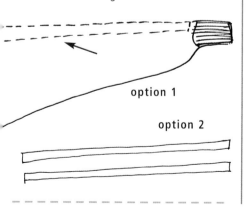

option 1

option 2

Tops

From the playing field to center stage, sweatshirts have a new identity. In this section, you will glam up your everyday sweatshirt into an unforgettable masterpiece.

scoop-neck top with wide sash

SKILL LEVEL: 1

REQUIRED TIME:

BY MACHINE:

½ HOUR

BY HAND:

1 HOUR

Too casual? We don't think so. The long-sleeve scoop with sash is a masterpiece. Shown here in olive green, we paired it with red/gold/black plaid high-waist slacks.

You can wear this style with a myriad of bottoms. The sash can also be made from other vintage items, such as a T-shirt, denim scraps, scarves, or leather—the list is endless. This shirt is flattering for most body types. The sash helps create a waistline, and the scoop neck flatters most face shapes.

Materials

STANDARD MATERIALS

Fabric scissors

Marking devices

Measuring devices

Quilting straight pins (or other heavy-duty straight pins)

Thread in matching or contrasting color

Iron and ironing board

Sewing machine and sewing machine needles (optional)

Handsewing needles

SPECIAL MATERIALS

One crew-neck sweatshirt, your size

1. Using iron, press sweatshirt. Lay sweatshirt flat, right side out, and fold in half along center front, matching shoulder and armhole seams. Using measuring and marking devices, mark cutting lines as follows (see page 12):

A (neckline) = 2 inches down from top edge of crew neck

B (waistline) = 9 to 10 inches down from cutting line A, equal to half front waist measurement

C (bodice bottom) = 3½ inches up from top of ribbing

D (dropped shoulder) = 6½ inches down from shoulder

E (waistline length) = half front waist measurement, plus ½-inch seam allowance

F (fitted sleeve) = 4½ inches from center fold of sleeve

G (sash) = 3½ inches from ribbing; 7 inch total from lower edge

H (sash points) = 3½ inches across width of sleeve

Mark cutting lines at neckline, bodice bottom, and along sleeve and side seam, as shown. Using scissors, cut along all cutting lines, through all layers.

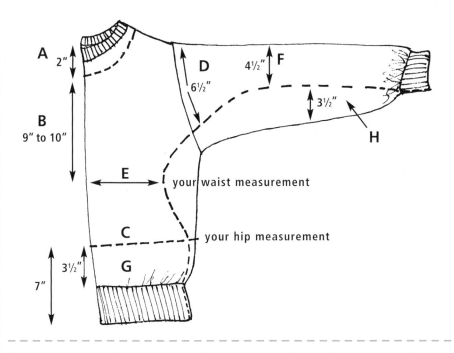

2. Turn top wrong side out and lay it flat, with front facing up. With right sides facing, pin front to back along sleeves and side seams, as shown. Stitch sleeve and side seams in direction indicated by arrows.

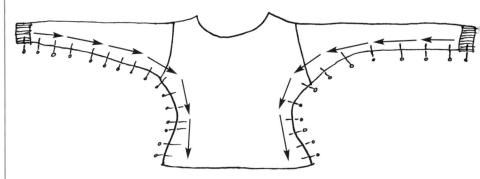

3. Trim long edges of two G pieces so each is approximately 7 inches wide. With right sides facing, lay two G pieces on top of each other. Pin and stitch at one short end. Lay joined G piece flat with right side facing up. Lay H pieces flat and right side up; trim so pieces measure 6 inches by 7 inches.

With right sides facing, pin one 7 inch edge of H piece to each end of the joined G piece, as shown. Stitch seams in direction indicated by arrows.

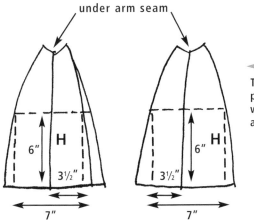

under arm seam

This is what your pieces look like when you open and lay them flat.

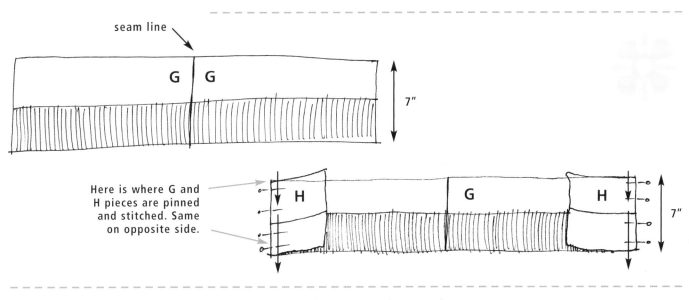

seam line

Here is where G and H pieces are pinned and stitched. Same on opposite side.

4. Lay long G piece (sash) flat and press seams open. Topstitch (see page 19) ¼ inch on each side of seams to keep seams flat, in direction indicated by arrows.

You can cut ends into points or leave straight.

Turn sweatshirt right side out and press. To wear, wrap sash around waist and tie.

Finished sash with possible sash points

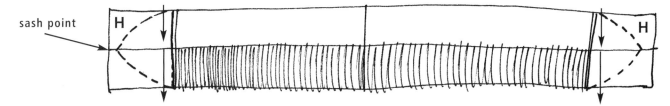

sash point

v-neck with sweater-knit sleeves

SKILL LEVEL: 1

REQUIRED TIME:

BY MACHINE:

1 HOUR

BY HAND:

2 HOURS

Refreshingly eclectic in its design, this revamped cinched sweatshirt with recycled sweater sleeves is easy to make. Shown here in vintage maroon sweatshirt fabric with boldly patterned sweater sleeves, this style is complementary to most body types. The V-neck gently frames the face and the subtle shaping makes the waist look smaller. Its open short sleeve gives it an edgy appeal. For some design options, change the sleeve fabric to a solid color, or gather the sleeves at the bottom for a more streamlined look.

Materials

STANDARD MATERIALS

Fabric scissors

Marking devices

Measuring devices

Quilting straight pins (or other heavy-duty straight pins)

Thread in matching or contrasting color

Iron and ironing board

Sewing machine and sewing machine needles (optional)

Handsewing needles

SPECIAL MATERIALS

One crew-neck sweatshirt, your size

One knit sweater, any size, any type (To avoid dry-cleaning, stick to cotton or synthetic knits. For more dramatic sleeves, choose an extra-large or man's sweater.)

1-inch-wide elastic, 7 inches

1. Using iron, press sweatshirt and sweater (if necessary). Put sweater aside. Lay sweatshirt flat, right side out, and fold in half along center front, matching shoulder and armhole seams. Pin together. Using measuring and marking devices, mark cutting lines as shown.

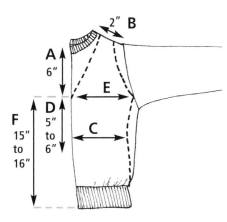

A (V neck) = 6 inches down center front from top of crew neck

B (shoulder) = 2 inches out on shoulder seam from V-neck line

C (waist level) = half front waist measurement, plus ¹/₂-inch seam allowance

D (center front to waist level) = point of V-neck is 5 to 6 inches up from waist level

E (bust level) = half front bust measurement, plus ¹/₂-inch seam allowance

F (center front to hem) = 15 to 16 inches down from point of V-neck

Mark diagonal cutting line from shoulder (B) to center front (A) to form V-neck. Mark curved armhole-cutting line from shoulder (B)

to bust level (E) at armhole. Mark curved side-seam cutting line from bust level at armhole to top of band, curving in at waistline (C). Using scissors, cut along all cutting lines through all fabric layers.

2a. Turn sweatshirt bodice wrong side out and lay flat with back facing up. Measure down from point of V-neck 8 to 9 inches and mark. Center ruler, horizontally, under mark. Measure out 4¹/₂ inches in each direction from mark. Mark these points.

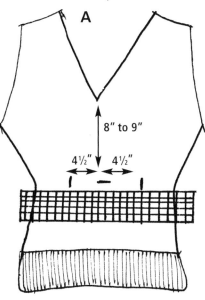

2b. Cut 7-inch length of 1-inch-wide elastic. Mark elastic at center and 1 inch in from each raw edge. Place elastic horizontally along waist, under marks, matching center of elastic to center mark on sweatshirt and side markings of elastic to corresponding side marks on sweatshirt (B). Pin in place. Machine stitch elastic to sweatshirt (see page 17).

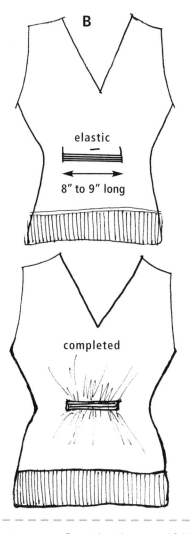

3. Lay sweater flat, right side out, and fold in half along center front, matching shoulder and armhole seams. Pin side seams together. Measure up center front 14 to 15 inches from bottom of hem and mark. Measure down side seam about 1 inch from armhole and mark. For sleeve cap, mark curved line across sweater from center front down to side seam, as shown. Mark cutting line along side seam. Cut along cutting lines, through all fabric layers. You will have two identical sweater fabric pieces (for sleeves).

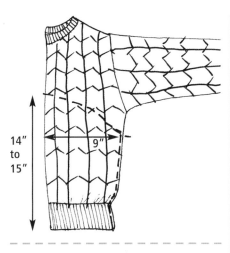

**14"
to
15"**

9"

4. Open two sleeve pieces (labeled A and B in illustration) and lay flat, right side facing up. Sew basting stitches (see pages 15 and 16) 1 inch from top edge, starting and ending 4 inches from each side edge, as shown.

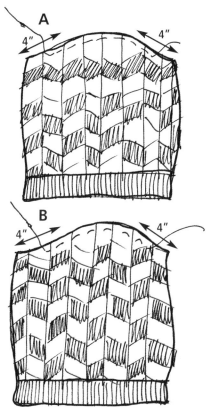

A

4"   4"

B

4"   4"

5. Gather sleeve tops by pulling basting threads in drawstring manner (see page 16).

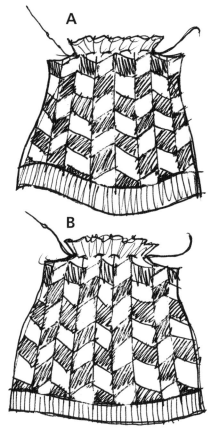

A

B

6. Lay bodice flat, right side facing up. With right sides facing, pin gathered edges of sleeves to armholes of bodice, centering sleeves in armholes, as shown. Note that edges of sleeves stop 3 ½ to 4 inches short of bottoms of armholes. Stitch sleeves to armholes in direction indicated by arrows. NOTE: Do not stitch underarm seams of sleeves.

7. Fold bodice at shoulder seams so right sides of front and back bodice are facing and pin side seams, as shown. Stitch side seams in direction indicated by arrows. NOTE: DO NOT stitch underarm seams of sleeves.

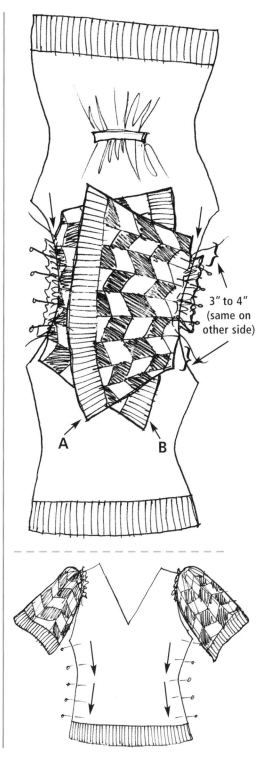

**3" to 4"
(same on
other side)**

A   **B**

fitted long-sleeve cardigan with snap ties

SKILL LEVEL: 2

REQUIRED TIME:

BY MACHINE:

½ HOUR

BY HAND:

1 HOUR

This new age cardigan is as cute as it is practical. The removable snap ties provide several styling options. Wear it opened or closed, with or without the ties. Here, we chose to revamp a vintage white sweatshirt with printed images on both the front and the back. We used metallic leather scraps as tie closures for ultimate pizzazz. It's a wonderful layering piece that you can wear with a multitude of options, such as tanks, tees, or turtlenecks.

Materials:

STANDARD MATERIALS

Fabric scissors

Marking devices

Measuring devices

Quilting straight pins (or other heavy-duty straight pins)

Thread in matching or contrasting color

Iron and ironing board

Sewing machine and sewing machine needles (optional)

Handsewing needles

SPECIAL MATERIALS

One crew-neck sweatshirt, your size

10 snaps (sew-on or non-sew), ½-inch size

1-inch-wide elastic, 7 inches

10-inch–by–6½-inch leather scrap (Recyle an old jacket, skirt, or pants from flea markets or used clothing shops.) See page 150 for leather-scrap sources.

1. Using iron, press sweatshirt. Lay sweatshirt flat, right side out, and fold in half along center front, matching shoulder and armhole seams. Using body measurements and measuring and marking devices, mark cutting lines, as shown.

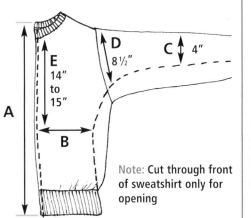

Note: **Cut through front of sweatshirt only for opening**

A (center front of cardigan) = On front only, mark from top of crew neck to bottom of ribbing.

B (waistline) = half front waist measurement, plus ½-inch seam allowance

C (fitted sleeve) = 4 inches from folded edge of sleeve

D (armhole) = 8½ inches down from top of shoulder

E (center front neck to waistline) = 14 to 15 inches

Mark cutting lines down center front and along sleeve and side seams, from bottom edge of sleeve ribbing to top of bodice ribbing, as shown. Using fabric scissors, cut along sleeve and side seam cutting lines *only*, through all fabric layers. Cut along center front cutting line *through front layer of sweatshirt only*.

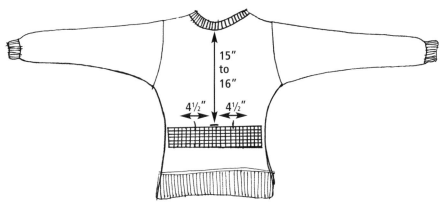

2. Lay sweatshirt flat, inside out, with back facing up. Beginning at neckline, measure down center back to waist level (about 15 to 16 inches). Mark. (You can also measure above or below waist level, depending on where you want the cinched waist to fall. We prefer the exact waist.)

Center ruler, horizontally, under mark. Measure out 4½ inches in each direction from mark. Mark these points.

3. Cut 7 inches length of 1-inch-wide elastic. Mark elastic at center and 1 inch in from each raw edge.

Place elastic horizontally along waist, under marks, matching center of elastic to center mark on sweatshirt and side markings of elastic to corresponding side marks on sweatshirt. Pin in place. Machine stitch elastic to sweatshirt (see page 17).

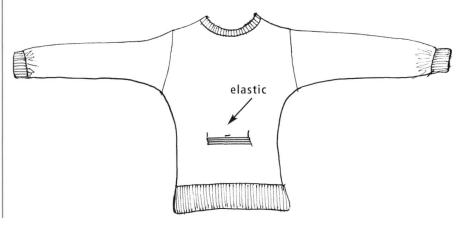

elastic

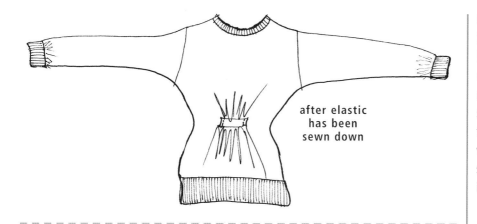

after elastic
has been
sewn down

6. For leather bows, cut 10-inch–by–6$\frac{1}{2}$-inch piece from scrap leather. Mark cutting lines every $\frac{3}{4}$ inches, as shown, and cut along cutting lines into ten $\frac{3}{4}$-inch strips. Mark snap placement at one end of each leather strip, about 1 inch from edge. (NOTE: Each of ten strips will be attached to cardigan front with snap. Cardigan will close by tying corresponding strip on each side of the center front into bow.)

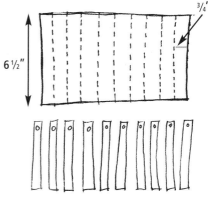

4. Leaving sweatshirt wrong side out, lay flat with front facing up. With right sides facing, pin front to back at underarms and side seams, as shown. Stitch seams in direction indicated by arrows. Press seams.

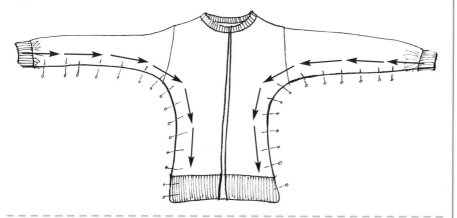

5. Turn sweatshirt right side out and lay flat with front facing up. Beginning 1 inch below neck band, mark snap placement for five snaps, marking every 4 inches on each side of center front, 1 inch from center front raw edges, as shown.

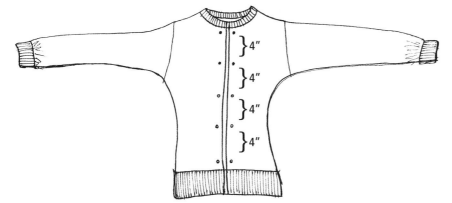

7. Attaching snaps: If using sew-on snaps, sew male part of snaps to cardigan at markings and sew female part of snaps to ten leather strips (see page 19).

If using non-sew snaps, follow manufacturer's instructions on package or find a shoe repair shop to attach snaps.

Once snaps are attached, snap leather strip to each snap on cardigan. Put the cardigan on and tie leather strips into bows, as shown in the photograph.

You can also wear the cardigan open, without leather strips. Snaps alone make an interesting trim on center front. NOTE: When washing cardigan, remove leather strips.

v-neck top with ruffled cap sleeves

SKILL LEVEL: 2

REQUIRED TIME:

BY MACHINE:

35 MINUTES

BY HAND:

1 HOUR

This flirty top is light and superfeminine. It transitions well in a myriad of social events—wear it to a barbecue, movie, or nightclub. Great for sweatshirts with favorite logos on the front, it looks adorable with shorts, skirts, and pants, from wide legs to cigarette cuts.

Materials

STANDARD MATERIALS

Fabric scissors

Marking devices

Measuring devices

Quilting straight pins (or other heavy-duty straight pins)

Thread in matching or contrasting color

Iron and ironing board

Sewing machine and sewing machine needles (optional)

Handsewing needles

SPECIAL MATERIALS

One crew-neck sweatshirt, your size

1. Using iron, press sweatshirt. Lay sweatshirt flat, right side out, and fold in half along center front, matching shoulder and armhole seams. Using measuring and marking devices, mark cutting lines using body measurements (see page 8) as shown.

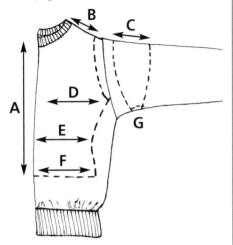

A (center front) = 15 to 17 inches, or center front length measurement

B (shoulder) = 2½ inches (not including neck-band ribbing)

C (sleeve cap) = 4 inches, beginning 1 inch in from shoulder seam

D (armhole level) = half front bust measurement, plus ½-inch seam allowance

E (waist level) = half front waist measurement, plus ½-inch seam allowance

F (hip level) = half front full hip measurement, plus ½-inch seam allowance

G (sleeve bottom) = 2 inches

Mark armhole cutting line from B to D. Mark side seam cutting line from D to F, curving in at waist (E). Mark sleeve cutting lines across sleeve from C to G. Using fabric scissors, cut along all cutting lines through all fabric layers. Put leftover sweatshirt pieces aside.

2. Finish raw edges of sweatshirt armholes (see page 44)

Open sweatshirt bodice and lay flat with wrong side facing up. NOTE: Front and back of bodice are in one piece, joined at shoulder seams and neck. Fold in half along center front and center back so right side is facing up, as shown. Mark cutting line around back neck band to shoulder seam, just outside neck band. Mark V-neck on front from shoulder seam to 6 to 7 inches down from center front neck. (If you want to be daring, measure down 8 inches.) Cut along all cutting lines through all fabric layers.

3. Lay sleeves flat; mark and cut notch at center top of each sleeve. Machine or hand baste (see pages 15 and 16) top of sleeve 1 inch from raw edge.

Pull basting threads in drawstring manner to gather sleeve tops, so they measure about 6 to 8 inches across (see page 16).

Cut bottom ribbing from sweatshirt and cut to length equal to bottom edge of bodice. Stitch short ends together in direction indicated by arrows.

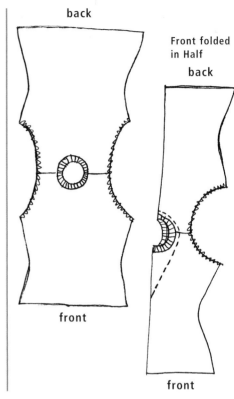

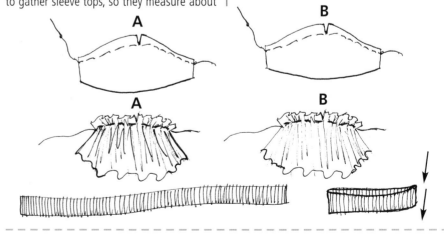

4. Lay bodice of sweatshirt flat with wrong side facing up. To hem armholes, fold up finished armhole edges ¼ to ½ inch, as shown; pin, then stitch hems.

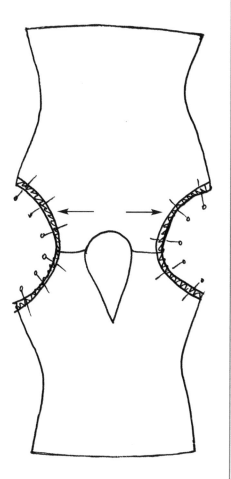

5. Lay bodice flat with right side facing up. With right sides facing, pin gathered edge of each sleeve to each armhole, matching sleeve notches to shoulder seams. Edges of sleeves will stop 3 ½ to 4 inches from edges of armholes, as shown. Stitch sleeves to armholes.

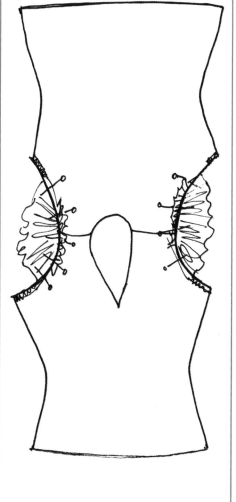

6. Fold bodice and sleeves at shoulder seams with right sides of front and back facing. Pin side seams and stitch side seams.

7. Using ribbing prepared in Step 3, pin ribbing to hem of bodice with right sides facing, as shown. Stitch ribbing to bodice. Press seam flat.

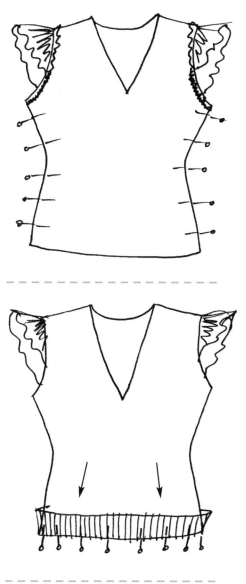

tube top with sequins and embellishments

SKILL LEVEL: 1

REQUIRED TIME:

BY MACHINE:

40 MINUTES

BY HAND:

1 ½ HOURS

This blinged-out tube top is a hot girl style. We encourage you to use a plethora of embellishments. We jazzed up this one with a red heart made from sweatshirt scraps. The sequins range from extra small to large, and we added Swarovski crystals and leaves made from leather scraps. This style is a great layering top; wear it over one of the three T's (tanks, tees, and turtlenecks) if you don't want to bare this much skin.

Materials

STANDARD MATERIALS

Fabric scissors

Marking devices

Measuring devices

Quilting straight pins (or other heavy-duty straight pins)

Thread in matching or contrasting color

Iron and ironing board

Sewing machine and sewing machine needles (optional)

Handsewing needles

SPECIAL MATERIALS

One crew-neck sweatshirt, M, L, or XL, depending on your bust size

Wax paper, plastic, or other material to use as glue barrier

Fabric glue (We recommend Aleene's Fabric Glue.)

Fabric or leather scraps (can be leftovers from other projects or old clothing, old gloves, etc.)

Decorative elements of your choice, such as sequins, beads, buttons, ribbons, or fabric paint

Cardboard, wax paper, plastic or other nonporous material, to act as a barrier to the glue

1. Using iron, press sweatshirt. Lay sweatshirt flat, right side out, with front facing up. Using measuring and marking devices, mark cutting line across front at armhole level. Mark parallel cutting line 10 to 11 inches below armhole level for midriff-baring top, or 15 to 16 inches down for waist-length top. Mark another cutting line just above ribbing, and final cutting line at side seam of ribbing, as shown. Cut along all cutting lines through all fabric layers. Cut off seam on one side of ribbing only. DO NOT cut side seams on body of sweatshirt.

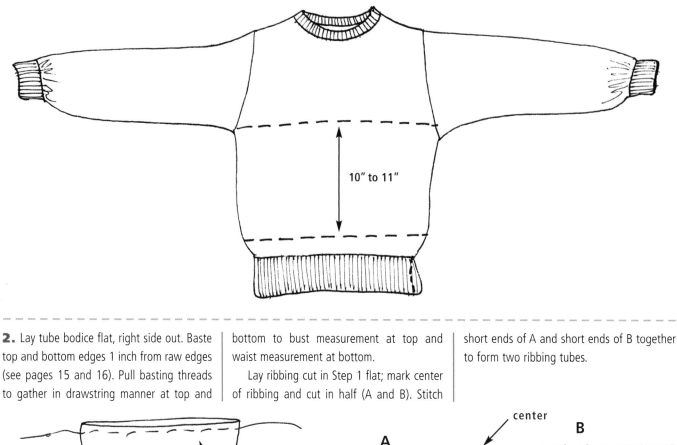

10" to 11"

2. Lay tube bodice flat, right side out. Baste top and bottom edges 1 inch from raw edges (see pages 15 and 16). Pull basting threads to gather in drawstring manner at top and bottom to bust measurement at top and waist measurement at bottom.

Lay ribbing cut in Step 1 flat; mark center of ribbing and cut in half (A and B). Stitch short ends of A and short ends of B together to form two ribbing tubes.

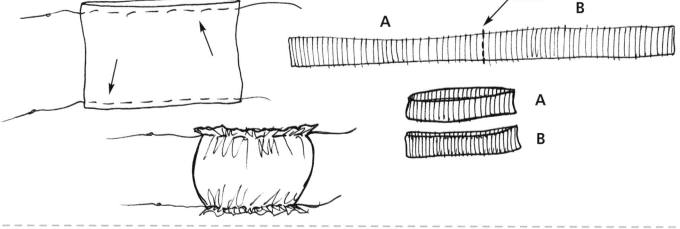

center

A   B

A

B

3. Lay tube bodice flat, right side out. Pin ribbing tube A to top edge of bodice and ribbing tube B to bottom edge of bodice with right sides facing, as shown, slightly stretching ribbing to fit bodice. Stitch ribbing to bodice in direction indicated by arrows. Turn right side out and press.

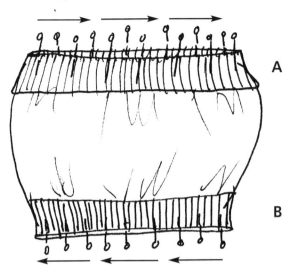

A

B

4. Using fabric scraps cut from T-shirts, sweatshirts, or leather, draw appliqué shapes on wrong side of scraps and cut out.

Lay bodice flat, right side out, with front facing up, and place cardboard, wax paper, plastic, or some other barrier inside bodice between front and back layers. This will prevent glue from leaking through to back of bodice. Arrange appliqués on front as you desire and glue in place. Once glue is dry, stitch appliqués to bodice along raw edges of each appliqué. For extra pizzazz, sew or glue on other decorative elements—such as sequins, beads, or ribbons—or decorate with fabric paints.

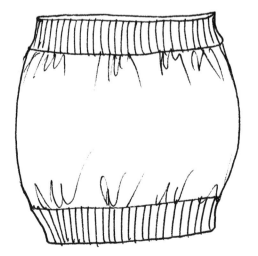

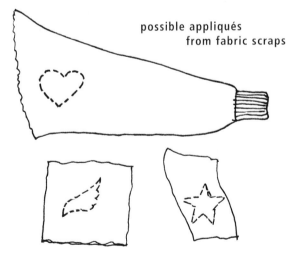

possible appliqués
from fabric scraps

Skirts

OUR SKIRTS FASHIONED FROM
SWEATSHIRTS HAVE PIZZAZZ AND FLAIR
TO SPARE. WITH STYLES THAT RANGE
FROM COMFORTABLY CUTE TO CUTTING-
EDGE EXCITING, AS FLATTERING AS
THEY ARE EASY TO WEAR, THESE SKIRTS
WILL UPLIFT A FLAT WARDROBE AND
TURN HEADS WITH THEIR ORIGINALITY.

bubble miniskirt with buttoned hem

SKILL LEVEL: 4

REQUIRED TIME:

BY MACHINE:

1 HOUR

BY HAND:

2 HOURS

Attention, all women in favor of showing legs, legs, and more legs—we vote this style for you. Made using a sweatshirt with a hand pouch, so you have a functional pocket, ours is a vintage forest-green sweatshirt with contrasting fuchsia buttonholes for extra kick.

For a more exaggerated puff on the skirt, button it up higher. Yes, you can make this skirt even shorter! (We have sewn secret buttons underneath the skirt for adjusting the length. You can also lengthen the skirt by adding length to the hemline when you cut it out.) Wear this bubble with printed or solid tights, leggings, or skinny jeans.

Materials

STANDARD MATERIALS

Fabric scissors

Marking devices (pens, pencils, chalk, or carbon paper)

Measuring devices (clear pattern ruler is best)

Quilting straight pins (or other heavy-duty straight pins)

Thread in matching or contrasting color

Iron and ironing board

Sewing machine and sewing machine needles (optional)

Handsewing needles

SPECIAL MATERIALS

One crew-neck sweatshirt with pocket pouch, size XXXL

Buttons, size of your choice

1. Using iron, press sweatshirt and lay it flat, right side up. Using body measurements (see page 8) and measuring and marking devices, mark cutting lines A to F, as shown (see page 12):

A (skirt front and back) = length: 14 to 16 inches (from bottom of armhole to top of ribbing); waistline (where A meets D): half of total waist measurement, plus 4 inches of ease; hemline: full width of sweatshirt, just above ribbing

B (skirt sides: center front/center back fold) = 14 to 16 inches down from shoulder seam (same measurement as skirt front and back length)

C (cutting line for bubble hem) = half lower hip measurement, plus 1 inch (if lower hip measurement is 38: 38 divided by 2 = 19, plus 1 inch = 20 inches for a 38-inch lower hip); 6 inches above line D

D (bubble hem) = 3 to 4 inches longer than line C

E (side seam of side skirt) = from underarm to length of B

F (skirt hip band) = entire ribbing

Mark waistline length on line D. Mark skirt front and back (A) cutting lines by drawing slightly curved side seam lines from skirt hemline to skirt waistline, as shown. Mark side skirt pieces by connecting B (side skirt fold line) to E (side skirt side seam), and then mark around armhole (hemline of side skirt).

Mark bubble hem cutting lines C (top) and D (bottom), as shown. Cut off entire ribbing (F) for hip band; cut off seam at one side to make one long piece.

Using scissors, cut along all cutting lines, through all fabric layers. NOTE: DO NOT cut along fold line of side skirt pieces (B). You will have two A pieces (skirt front and skirt back), two B pieces (side skirts), two D pieces (bubble hem), and one F piece (ribbing hip band).

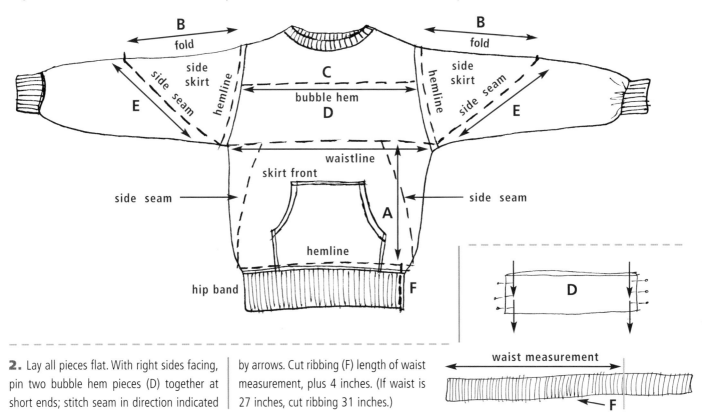

2. Lay all pieces flat. With right sides facing, pin two bubble hem pieces (D) together at short ends; stitch seam in direction indicated by arrows. Cut ribbing (F) length of waist measurement, plus 4 inches. (If waist is 27 inches, cut ribbing 31 inches.)

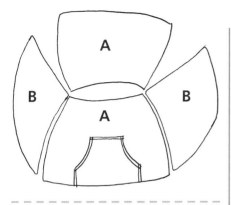

3. Lay all four skirt pieces (two A and two B) flat. With right sides together, pin side seam edges of skirt side pieces (B) to side seam edges of skirt front, as shown. Stitch seams in direction indicated by arrows. Then pin and sew the other side seams to the back. NOTE: Skirt front is piece A with pouch pocket.

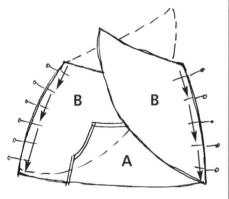

4. Lay skirt flat, wrong side up, and machine or hand baste ½ inch away from raw edge of skirt bottom (see page 16).

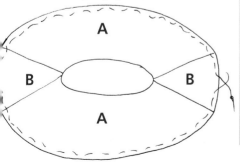

Pull basting threads in drawstring manner to gather bottom of skirt, as shown (see page 16). Turn right side out.

5. With right sides facing, pin ribbing (F) to skirt at waistline, and bubble hem (D) to skirt at hemline. Adjusting gathers to fit, stitch seams in direction indicated by arrows. Press seams flat.

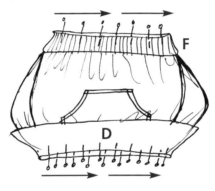

6. Turn skirt wrong side out and lay flat. Turn bottom edge of bubble hem up the width of buttons, plus ½ inch. Press. Stitch ¼ inch from raw edge. (You have just made the buttonhole placket.) Turn skirt right side out and lay flat. Mark buttonhole placement on placket (see pages 20 and 21), as shown. NOTE: Space buttonholes 2 to 3 inches apart. Stitch buttonholes and cut buttonhole openings (see page 21).

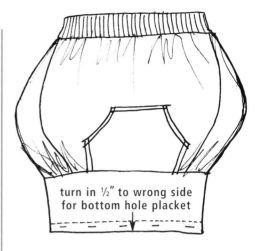

turn in ½" to wrong side for bottom hole placket

7. Turn skirt wrong side out. Fold entire bubble hem up toward skirt. Mark button placement through buttonhole openings onto skirt, as shown (A). Fold bubble hem down and sew buttons at markings. (Buttons are on the wrong side, the inside, of the skirt [B].) You can wear skirt with bubble hem buttoned or unbuttoned.

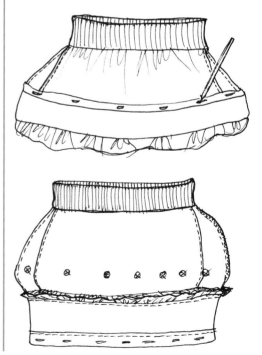

triangle skirt with side ruffle

SKILL LEVEL: 1

REQUIRED TIME:

BY MACHINE:

20 MINUTES

BY HAND:

45 MINUTES

Who would have thought to describe a sweatshirt as romantic? This triangle skirt with raw edges and side ruffle is full of grace. Shown here in olive-green sweat fabric, this design works well in a sophisticated, upscale environment.

Accompany this skirt with a silk blouse, button-front blouse, or turtleneck (as pictured). For a more casual look, you can sport this skirt up with tanks and tees.

Materials

STANDARD MATERIALS
Fabric scissors

Marking devices

Measuring devices

Quilting straight pins (or other heavy-duty straight pins)

Thread in matching or contrasting color

Iron and ironing board

Sewing machine and sewing machine needles (optional)

Handsewing needles

SPECIAL MATERIALS
One crew-neck sweatshirt with logo, size L or XL

Carmen: This is one of my favorite styles. I love that it's coquettish and feminine. The ruffle makes me feel like I'm in England at high tea.

1. Using iron, press sweatshirt. Lay sweatshirt flat, right side out, with front facing up. Using body measurements (see page 8) and measuring and marking devices, mark cutting lines A to D, as shown (see page 12).

A (skirt waist) = half waist measurement, plus 8 to 10 inches, depending on length of drape desired (30-inch waist divided by 2 = 15 inches + 8 to 10 inches)

B (skirt side) = entire length of sweatshirt

C (skirt hem) = entire width of sweatshirt, just above ribbing

D (waistband) = entire ribbing

Using fabric scissors, cut along all cutting lines through all fabric layers.

NOTE: DO NOT cut sweat along unmarked side seam.

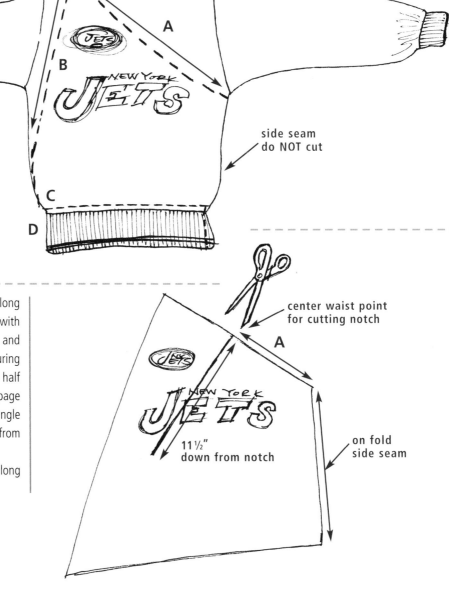

side seam
do NOT cut

center waist point
for cutting notch

A

11½"
down from notch

on fold
side seam

2. With wrong sides facing, fold skirt along intact side seam. Lay folded skirt flat with front facing up, waistline A at the top, and folded side seam on the right. Measuring from right to left, mark a point equal to half waist measurement and cut notch (see page 15). Draw line perpendicular or at right angle to waist, extending 11½ inches down from notch, as shown.

Stitch skirt front and back together, along this line.

3. Lay ribbing flat. Mark full waist measurement (A); cut. Lay ribbing equal to waist measurement flat (B). Fold ribbing in half and stitch short raw edges together (C) in direction indicated by arrows.

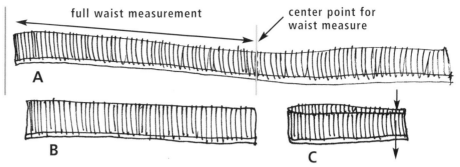

4. Turn skirt right side out with waist at top. Turn ribbing waistband right side out. Slip ribbing waistband over skirt waist (wrong side of ribbing facing right side of skirt), overlapping raw edge of band 1 inch over skirt. Pin and topstitch (see page 19) ribbing to skirt in direction indicated by arrows.

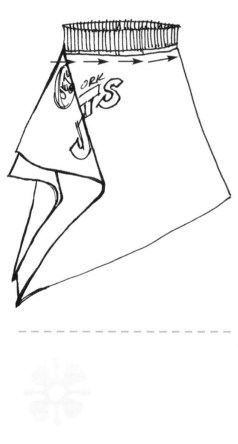

wrap skirt with sash

REQUIRED TIME:

BY MACHINE:

1 HOUR

BY HAND:

2 HOURS

Playing on the classic wrap dress, we converted the old-school sweat into a fashion-forward wrap skirt. At Sistahs of Harlem, we like versatility—the ability to wear clothing in numerous environments—and this skirt delivers. Wear it with the top of your choice, from casual to office to night on the town. Pictured here in vintage white sweat fabric with a green sash, this wrap skirt is an easy wear and a wardrobe staple.

Materials

STANDARD MATERIALS

Fabric scissors

Marking devices

Measuring devices

Quilting straight pins (or other heavy-duty straight pins)

Thread in matching or contrasting color

Iron and ironing board

Sewing machine and sewing machine needles (optional)

Handsewing needles

SPECIAL MATERIALS

Two crew-neck sweatshirts, size X or XL

puffed-leg shorts

SKILL LEVEL: 3

REQUIRED TIME:

BY MACHINE:

1 HOUR

BY HAND:

2 HOURS

The puff shorts are as comfortable as they are eye-catching. Intertwining the sporty and the glamorous, this is a style for those who want to showcase their legs. The wrap sash is a special detail that helps define the waist. Wear the puff shorts to the gym or to the park. They can be upgraded to a supersassy ensemble with a sophisticated top, as pictured.

Materials

STANDARD MATERIALS

Fabric scissors

Marking devices

Measuring devices

Quilting straight pins (or other heavy-duty straight pins)

Thread in matching or contrasting color

Iron and ironing board

Sewing machine and sewing machine needles (optional)

Handsewing needles

SPECIAL MATERIALS

One pair sweatpants, one size larger than your size

One sweatshirt, size L or XL, or ribbing from one sweatshirt

Two buttons, any size

1. Using iron, press sweatpants and sweatshirt. Put sweatshirt aside. Lay sweatpants flat, right side out with front facing up. Using body measurements (see page 8) and measuring and marking devices, mark cutting lines (see page 12), as shown:

A (shorts front and back) = horizontal top line: front waist measurement; bottom horizontal lines: 3 inches below crotch level, across entire width of legs (or more than 3 inches below crotch level if longer shorts are desired); left-side cutting lines, as shown; right-side *curved* cutting line, as shown

B (waistband) = 4 inches by 30 to 33 inches (depending on waist measurement)

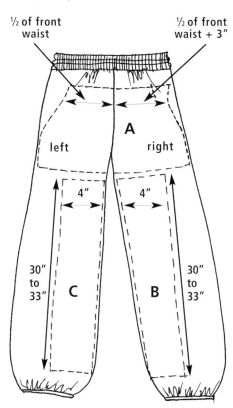

½ of front waist

½ of front waist + 3"

left

right

A

4"   4"

30" to 33"   C   B   30" to 33"

C (ties) = 4 inches by 30 to 33 inches (depending on waist measurement and desired length of ties)

Using fabric scissors, cut along all cutting lines through all fabric layers.

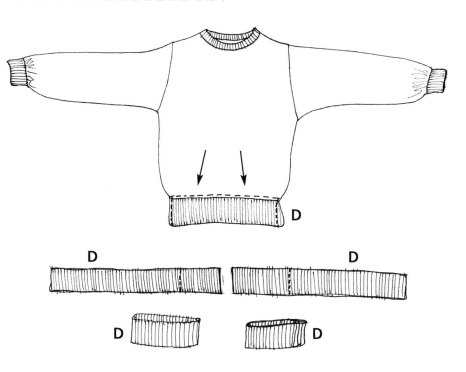

D

D   D

D   D

2. Lay sweatshirt flat, right side out with front facing up. Cut ribbing (**D**) off bottom of sweatshirt body. Cut ribbing into two equal lengths. Pin each ribbing piece together at short ends and stitch seam. You will have two ribbing "circles" for ribbing hems at bottom of shorts. Put aside.

3. With right sides facing and shorts front on top, pin front to back, matching side seams, as shown. NOTE: Begin pinning and stitching on right side seam 3 to 4 inches below waistline. Stitch seams on both sides.

On side of shorts front with open side seam, mark and cut notches (see page 15) into waistline of front and back, 3 to 4 inches from unsewn edge.

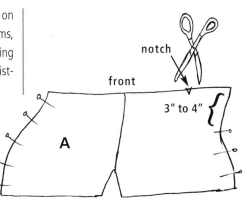

notch

front

3" to 4"

A

4. Pin two C pieces and two B pieces together at short ends; stitch seams in direction indicated by arrows. Pin joined C pieces (ties) to each end of joined B pieces (waistband); stitch. Press seams flat. Set aside.

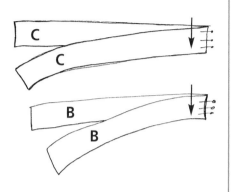

5. Optional back darts: If you want a looser fit in back, skip darts. With wrong side out, flip shorts over so back side is facing up. Measure out 3 inches from each side of center back; mark. Draw dart lines from marks down 3 ½ inches from waist. Sew darts (see page 20).

Sew basting stitch (see pages 15 and 16) at bottom of each leg. Pull basting thread in drawstring manner to gather shorts at hem (see page 16). Gathered bottom should equal thigh circumference at widest part of thigh.

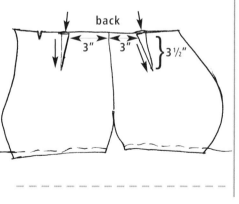

6. On one open side seam (at left), mark two horizontal buttonholes (see pages 20 and 21), 1 ½ inches apart. Stitch buttonholes and cut buttonhole opening (see page 21). On opposite open side seam, mark button placement through buttonhole openings. (You'll sew buttons in Step 9.)

7. Turn shorts right side out and lay flat with front facing up. With right sides facing, pin waistband/tie (made in Step 3) to waist, *beginning and ending* at notches on waistline. Stitch waistband to shorts in directions indicated by arrows, leaving ends of ties loose. NOTE: DO NOT stitch seam beyond notches.

8. With shorts right side out and front facing up, pin ribbing (made in Step 2) to bottom of each leg, over gathering. Stretch ribbing

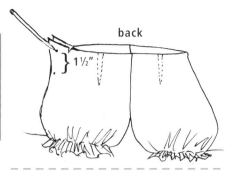

slightly to fit gathered leg. Stitch ribbing to leg. Press seam flat.

Optional: Trim each waistband/tie, as shown, from notch on waistline, for about 6 or 7 inches. This will make the tie less bulky when knotted.

9. Turn shorts right side out and press. Sew buttons at markings.

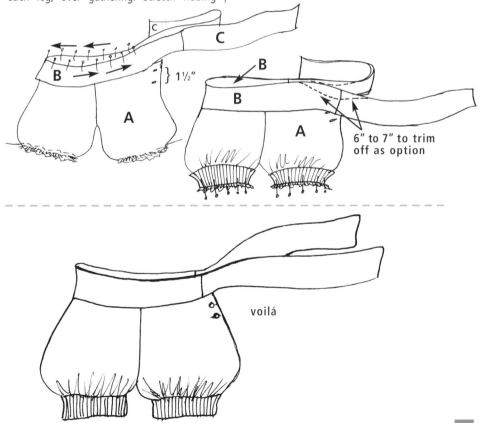

Dresses

These dresses were created to be
flat-out showstoppers. From maxi
length to mini, the sweatshirt
dress pushes cosmopolitan style
to the next level.

pullover baby doll top or dress

SKILL LEVEL: 2

REQUIRED TIME:

BY MACHINE:

45 MINUTES

BY HAND:

1½ HOURS

This style is an all-time favorite of ours. The supercute baby doll top is flirty sweet. Pictured here in vintage purple Champion sweatshirt fabric, this style can be worn with jeans, slacks, tights, bicycle shorts, or leggings. We chose cobalt-blue metallic leggings in homage to the disco era! And you don't have to wear it as a mini; just cut the skirt to any length you desire.

Note: *If you are over 5'9", this garment will fit more like a top than a dress.*

and Note: *Take very accurate measurements from the shoulder to beneath the breast—this will be your G measurement. You want to make sure that the empire bustline hits beneath the bust and not on or over it.*

Materials

STANDARD MATERIALS

Fabric scissors

Marking devices

Measuring devices

Quilting straight pins (or other heavy-duty straight pins)

Thread in matching or contrasting color

Iron and ironing board

Sewing machine and sewing machine needles (optional)

Handsewing needles

SPECIAL MATERIALS

One crew-neck sweatshirt, size XXL to XXXL (or two smaller crew necks)

¼-inch-wide elastic, 16 to 20 inches

1. Using iron, press sweatshirt. Lay sweatshirt flat, right side out, and fold in half along center front, matching shoulder and armhole seams. Using your body measurements (see page 8) and measuring and marking devices, mark cutting lines, as shown (see page 12):

A (bodice bust level) = half front bust measurement, plus $\frac{1}{2}$-inch seam allowance

B (skirt) = 17 to 19 inches or longer from G

C (sleeve at shoulder) = 8 inches from shoulder seam

D (sleeve at underarm) = 6 inches from armhole seam

E (armhole level) = 7 to 8 inches from top of neck band

F (shoulder seam) = 2 inches, including neck band

G (bodice bottom edge) = 9 to 10 inches from top of neck band or longer if you desire; see note on page 100.

H (sleeve hem) = 7 to 8 inches across sleeve

Mark bodice cutting lines: armhole from F to A, side seam from A to G, and hemline at G level.

Mark sleeve cutting lines: sleeve cap from C to D, and hem (H).

Using fabric scissors, cut along all cutting lines, through all fabric layers.

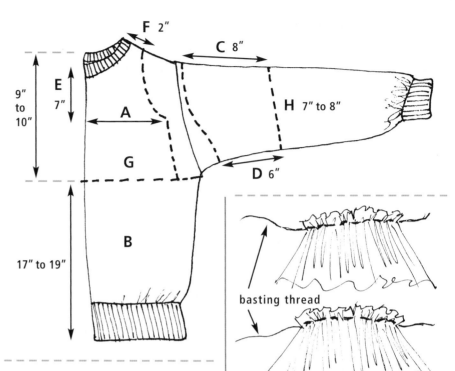

2. Separate sleeves and lay flat. Notch each sleeve at center top of sleeve curve. Hand or machine baste (see pages 15 and 16) 1 inch from top edge of each sleeve. Pull basting thread in drawstring manner to gather sleeve top (see page 16).

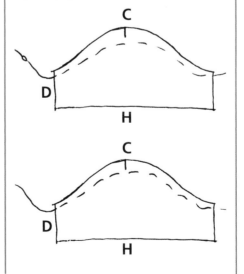

basting thread

3. Lay bodice flat with right side facing up. NOTE: Front and back of bodice are in one piece, joined at shoulder seams and neck. With right sides facing in, pin gathered edge of each sleeve to each armhole, matching

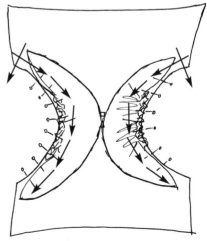

sleeve notches to shoulder seams, adjusting gathered edges of sleeves to fit armholes. Stitch sleeves to armholes in direction indicated by arrows.

- -

4. Fold bodice and sleeves at shoulder seams, so right sides of front and back are facing each other. Pin side seams and stitch in direction indicated by arrows.

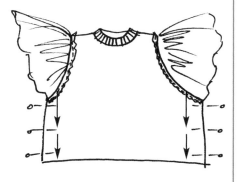

5. Turn bodice right side out and lay flat with front of bodice facing up. With right sides facing, slide skirt (B, cut in Step 1) over bodice, matching bottom edge of band on skirt to bottom edge of bodice and pin, as shown. Note: You will not see the bodice once you slide the skirt over it. The illustration shows the bodice so you can see where and how to join the skirt and bodice. Stitch skirt to bodice.

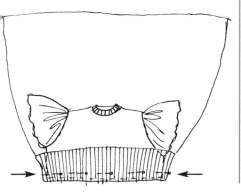

6. Turn dress right side out, and check bodice/skirt seam, making sure seam has been sewn properly around entire garment.

- -

7. Turn dress wrong side out. Cut two 8-to-10-inch lengths of $1/4$-inch-wide elastic. Stitch one length of elastic to bottom of each sleeve (see page 17), about $1/2$ inch from raw edge of sleeve, in the direction indicated by arrows.

Turn dress right side out and press.

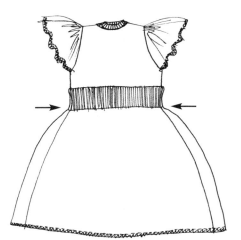

v-neck maxi dress with asymmetrical hem

SKILL LEVEL: 1

REQUIRED TIME:

BY MACHINE:
1 ½ HOURS

BY HAND SEWING:
2 ½ HOURS

Take center stage in this long-sleeve maxi-length dress with a deep V-neck and asymmetrical hemline. Designed with the bodice in white and the skirt in purple and orange, the complementary colors highlight the dramatic asymmetrical hemline. You can reinterpret this dress in a monochromatic color palette for a simpler, more understated look. It's so easy, you can make two.

Materials

STANDARD MATERIALS

Fabric scissors

Marking devices

Measuring devices

Quilting straight pins (or other heavy-duty straight pins)

Thread in matching or contrasting color

Iron and ironing board

Sewing machine and sewing machine needles (optional)

Handsewing needles

SPECIAL MATERIALS

One crew-neck sweatshirt with front pocket, size L to XL
(for dress bodice)

Two crew-neck sweatshirts in contrasting or complementary colors
to above, size L to XL (for dress skirt)

1. Using iron, press the three sweatshirts. Lay sweatshirt with pocket flat, right side out, front facing up. Using body measurements (see page 8) and measuring and marking devices, mark cutting line (see page 12) just above ribbing at bottom edge. Using half of waist measurement, plus 1½ inches, mark on each side of sweatshirt, just above top of patch pocket. Mark cutting line on each side of sweatshirt from ribbing, up side and sleeves, about 2 to 3 inches inside of side seams (depending on your waist measurement), curving in slightly at waist mark, as shown. Sleeve cutting lines should be 8 inches at armhole seams and 5 inches at wrist. Total sleeve length should be 18 to 23 inches, depending on arm length.

Cut along all cutting lines through all fabric layers.

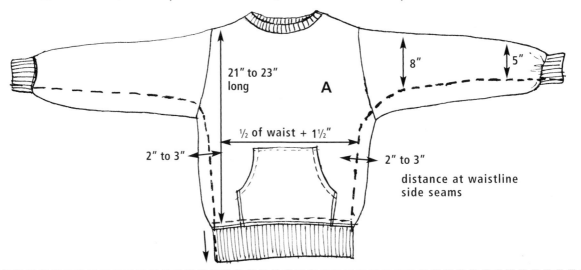

2. Lay one sweatshirt (without pocket) flat, right side out with front facing up. Beginning at where shoulder seam meets neck band, measure one diagonal cutting line, 21 to 23 inches long, down side seam to ribbing, and another diagonal cutting line across shirt to just under armhole, 20 to 22 inches long. Mark cutting line just above ribbing and along side seam. Cut along all cutting lines through all fabric layers. You have two B pieces. With right sides facing, pin B pieces at side seam. Stitch side seam; press seam flat. This is the upper skirt.

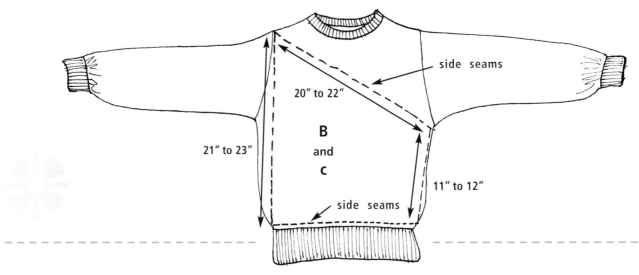

3. Mark and cut the other sweatshirt without the pocket as you did in Step 2, to create two C pieces. With right sides facing, pin C pieces at side seam. Stitch side seam; press seam flat. This is the lower skirt.

4. Lay bodice with pocket cut in Step 1 flat with wrong side facing up. NOTE: Front and back bodice are joined at shoulder seams. Fold in half along center front and back, matching side seam and sleeve edges, so right side is facing up, as shown. Mark cutting line just inside neck band on back, and V-neck cutting line, about 6 inches down from center front neck band. Cut along cutting lines through all fabric layers.

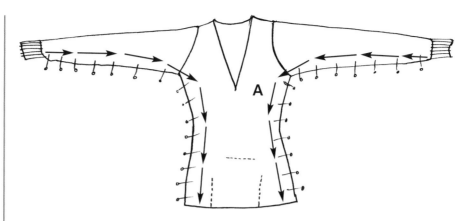

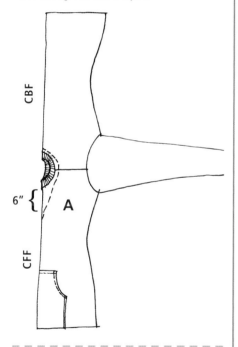

5. Open bodice and lay flat. With right sides facing and bodice front facing up, pin bodice front to bodice back at side seams and underarm seams. Stitch seams in direction indicated by arrows.

6. Turn bodice right side out and lay flat with front facing up. With right sides facing, pin longest edge of upper skirt (B), to bottom of bodice, matching side seam of skirt B to one side seam of bodice. Begin pinning at bodice/skirt side seam, working from side seam to side seam across front and from side seam to side seam across back. NOTE: Skirt will be longer than bodice, with excess fabric on one side of bodice, as shown. Press seam flat.

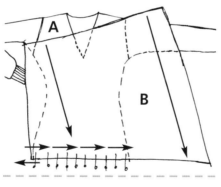

7. Turn bodice and upper skirt right side out with front facing up. Overlap top edge of lower skirt (C), over bottom edge of upper skirt (B), with wrong side of lower skirt facing right side of upper skirt. Pin, then topstitch (or whipstitch) two skirt layers together, as shown.

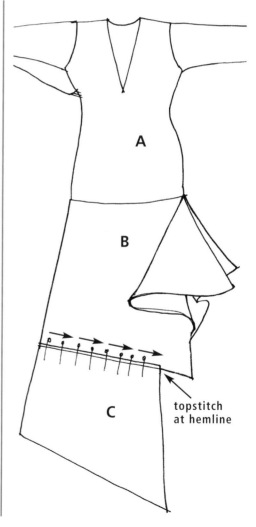

topstitch at hemline

scoop-neck minidress with ruffle trim

SKILL LEVEL: 2

REQUIRED TIME:

BY MACHINE:

40 MINUTES

BY HAND:

1½ HOURS

We are big fans of mixing fabric textures. This design showcases a sassy combination of sweatshirting and cotton shirting to create a saucy, short-sleeve, scoop-neck minidress, adorned with random ruffles. It's made from a vintage navy Russell athletic sweatshirt; the crisp, white ruffles with pinked edges are randomly placed on the hips. It's a dynamic look. You can make the ruffles using fabric from men's shirting (our favorite) or from whatever you choose. Wear this as a long tunic if you don't want to reveal so much leg.

Materials

STANDARD MATERIALS

Fabric scissors

Marking devices

Measuring devices

Quilting straight pins (or other heavy-duty straight pins)

Thread in matching or contrasting color

Iron and Ironing board

Sewing machine and sewing machine needles (optional)

Handsewing needles

SPECIAL MATERIALS

Pinking shears

One crew-neck sweatshirt, one or two sizes larger than you wear

One sleeve from man's dress shirt

   (We suggest you use a shirt with bright stripes.)

sliced-sleeve mini with leather appliqués

· · · · · · · · · · · ·

SKILL LEVEL: 1

REQUIRED TIME:

BY MACHINE:

40 MINUTES

BY HAND:

1 HOUR

We can't help it. Again, we pay homage to the *Flashdance* era, the '80s! Here's an updated twist on the sultry sweatshirt dress. This short-sleeve, scoop-neck dress with slashed sleeves is a blank canvas for embellishment, and we adorned ours with an array of sequins, leather patches, and Swarovski crystals; or use decorative buttons, handpainting, or airbrushing to bring out your inner Andy Warhol. *Flashdance* glam is still awesome.

Materials

STANDARD MATERIALS

Fabric scissors

Marking devices

Measuring devices

Quilting straight pins (or other heavy-duty straight pins)

Thread in matching or contrasting color

Iron and Ironing board

Sewing machine and sewing machine needles (optional)

Handsewing needles

SPECIAL MATERIALS

One crew-neck sweatshirt, one to two sizes larger than you wear

Fabric scraps for appliqués (any type of fabric, including leather)

Crystals for embellishing appliqués (or beads, sequins,
   or other sparkle elements)

Fabric glue (We recommend Aleene's Fabric Glue.)

Cardboard, wax paper, plastic, or other nonporous material,
   to act as a barrier to the glue.

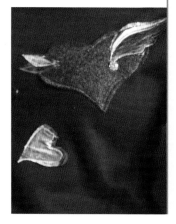

1. Using iron, press sweatshirt. Lay sweatshirt flat, right side out, and fold in half along center front, matching shoulder and armhole seams. Using body measurements (see page 8) and measuring and marking devices, mark cutting lines (see page 12) as shown.

A (center front) = 22 to 23 inches, or your center front length (this will be length of dress)

B (armhole level) = half front bust measurement, plus $\frac{1}{2}$-inch seam allowance, about halfway between waistline and shoulder

C (waist level) = half front waist measurement, plus $\frac{1}{2}$-inch seam allowance, about halfway between armhole level and hip

D (hip level) = half front natural hip, plus $\frac{1}{2}$-inch seam allowance, $\frac{1}{2}$ inch above bottom ribbing (about 8 to 9 inches below waistline)

E (shoulder) = 2 $\frac{1}{2}$ inches

F (neckline) = 2 inches below neck-band ribbing

G/I (sleeve length) = 5 $\frac{1}{2}$ inches

H/J (sleeve width) = across entire width of sleeve

Mark armhole cutting line from E to B. Mark side seam cutting line from B through C to D. Mark neckline cutting line F. Mark sleeve cap (J) from top of G to top of I, then sleeve hemline H.

On sleeve, beginning $\frac{1}{2}$ inch from shoulder seam (G), measure down 5 $\frac{1}{2}$ inches on

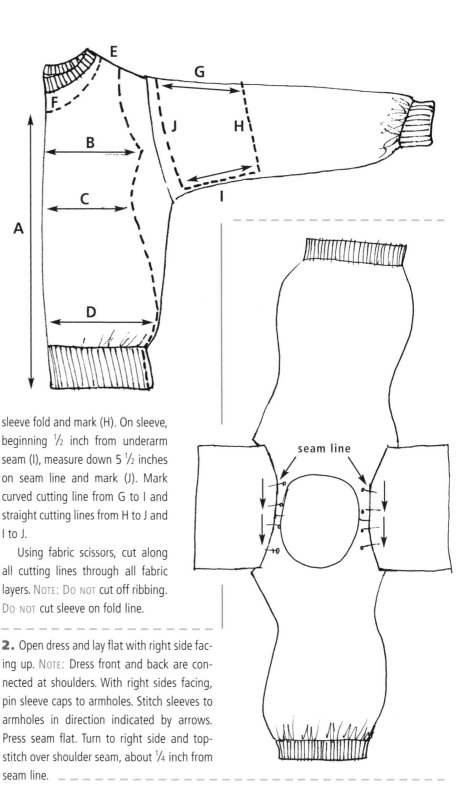

sleeve fold and mark (H). On sleeve, beginning $\frac{1}{2}$ inch from underarm seam (I), measure down 5 $\frac{1}{2}$ inches on seam line and mark (J). Mark curved cutting line from G to I and straight cutting lines from H to J and I to J.

Using fabric scissors, cut along all cutting lines through all fabric layers. NOTE: DO NOT cut off ribbing. DO NOT cut sleeve on fold line.

2. Open dress and lay flat with right side facing up. NOTE: Dress front and back are connected at shoulders. With right sides facing, pin sleeve caps to armholes. Stitch sleeves to armholes in direction indicated by arrows. Press seam flat. Turn to right side and topstitch over shoulder seam, about $\frac{1}{4}$ inch from seam line.

3. With right sides facing, pin dress front to dress back at side seams. Stitch side seams in direction indicated by arrows.

NOTE: DO NOT sew underarm seams on sleeves. Press all seams flat.

4. Decorate dress with appliqué designs. Using fabric scraps from your stash, draw or trace appliqué designs (as many and as varied as you like) directly onto fabric; cut out appliqué shapes. Arrange appliqué shapes on dress as you desire, then glue in place. NOTE: Be sure to put wax paper or another barrier inside dress, between back and front, to pre-vent glue from leaking through and adhering front to back. When glue is dry, stitch appliqués to dress close to appliqué edges. Optional: If you know how to embroider, use embroidery stitch(es) of your choice around outside edges of appliqués. Decorate appliqués with beads, buttons, sequins, bugle beads, etc., glued or sewn in place.

completed dress with
possible appliqués

Accessories

Sweatshirts make awesome accessories! Each style adds finesse to a complete ensemble. The extra punch from these accessory projects knock the sweat off—no pun intended!

appliquéd mittens with ribbons

SKILL LEVEL: 1

REQUIRED TIME:

BY MACHINE

½ HOUR

BY HAND:

45 MINUTES TO

1 HOUR

No one wants cold hands in the winter. These delightful sweatshirt mittens are not only practical but also extremely easy to make. To the basic gray sweatshirt fabric, we added a favorite SOH embellishment—the leather leaf. Adorned with small paillettes and grosgrain ribbon bows at the wrists, this style was created out of necessity. A friend and I were going ice-skating at Rockefeller Center on a bitter cold January day, and I couldn't find my gloves. Grabbing an old sweatshirt, I traced my hand on it and with some quick handsewing and a piece of leftover ribbon, in practically no time at all I had hand coverings that were warmer and more stylish than my gloves. You could also line your mittens with fleece for increased warmth.

Materials

STANDARD MATERIALS

Fabric scissors

Marking devices

Measuring devices

Quilting straight pins (or other heavy-duty straight pins)

Thread in matching or contrasting color

Iron and ironing board

Sewing machine and sewing machine needles (optional)

Handsewing needles

SPECIAL MATERIALS

Two sweatshirt sleeves in same color, size L or larger

Sweatshirt scraps or sleeve in contrasting color

Ribbon, two lengths, each ½ inch by 20 inches

Sequins, crystals, buttons, or beads for embellishments

Fabric glue (We recommend Aleene's Fabric Glue.)

Cardboard, wax paper, plastic, or other nonporous material,
   to act as a barrier to the glue.

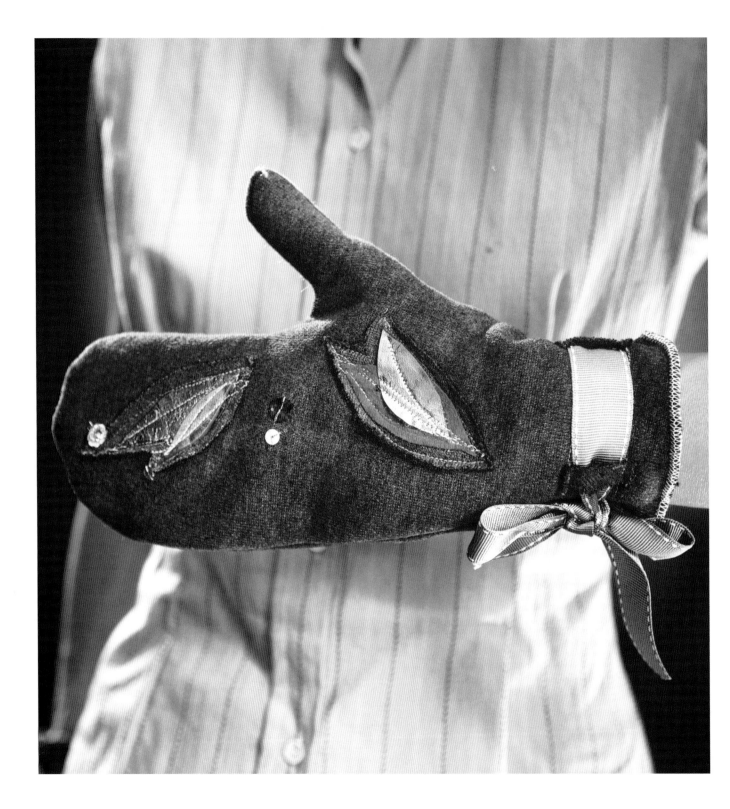

1. Open up seam line of two same-color sweatshirt sleeves. Using iron, press each and lay flat on top of one another. Place left hand flat on sleeve and, using marking device, trace around hand about 1 inch away from hand. Repeat procedure for right hand. Mark four strips, about $1/4$ inch by 2 inches, to be used as loops for threading ribbons.

On contrasting sweatshirt scraps or sleeve, mark appliqué designs (leaves, hearts, stars, or any shape you like). Using fabric scissors, cut along all cutting lines through all fabric layers.

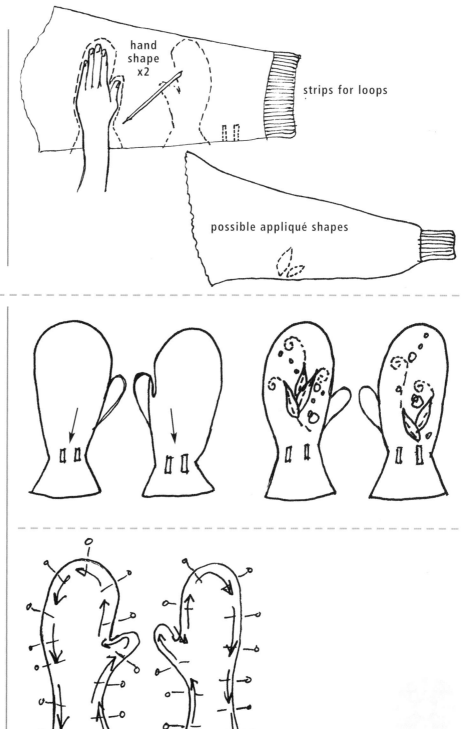

hand shape x2

strips for loops

possible appliqué shapes

2. Lay four mitten pieces flat. Stitch or glue two small fabric strips to each mitten piece at wrist level for ribbon loops. NOTE: Place wax paper or other barrier under mitten pieces to prevent glue from leaking through and adhering mittens to working surface.

Arrange appliqué designs on two mitten pieces and glue in place. When glue is dry, stitch appliqués to mittens close to appliqué edges. Optional: If desired, use embroidery stitches of your choice around outside edges of appliqués. Using fabric glue, embellish appliqués with sequins, crystals, buttons, beads, etc., gluing in place.

3. With rights sides facing, pin one embellished mitten piece to one plain mitten piece, leaving bottom edge free, as shown. Stitch mitten together in direction indicated by arrows. Finish lower edge on mitten as desired using a serger or whipstitch finish (see page 20).

Turn mittens right side out. Lace ribbons through loops and tie in bow.

armwarmers with satin ribbon laces

SKILL LEVEL: 1

REQUIRED TIME:

BY MACHINE

½ HOUR

BY HAND:

45 MINUTES TO

1 HOUR

Wear short sleeves in colder climates without a problem. With the help of these fun pieces, you can wear your arm-baring shirts and not feel chilled. They make great layering pieces—throw them on top of long-sleeve tees, turtlenecks, and blouses. Swap out the satin ties with cord, leather, or lace. These armwarmers are phenomenal accessories, adding élan to an ordinary ensemble.

Materials

STANDARD MATERIALS

Fabric scissors

Marking devices

Measuring devices

Quilting straight pins (or other heavy-duty straight pins)

Thread in matching or contrasting color

Iron and ironing board

Sewing machine and sewing machine needles (optional)

Handsewing needles

SPECIAL MATERIALS

Two sweatshirt sleeves, size L or larger

Satin ribbon, two lengths, each 1 inch by 60-plus inches

1. Press sweatshirt sleeves and lay flat. Using body measurements (see page 8) and measuring and marking devices, on each sleeve mark (see page 12) vertical cutting lines A (half upper arm measurement, plus 1 inch) and horizontal cutting line B (arm length, 24 to 26 inches, including cuff ribbing).

On each sleeve, mark four small strips, about ¼ inch by 2 inches, to be used as loops for threading ribbons.

Using fabric scissors, cut along all cutting lines through all fabric layers.

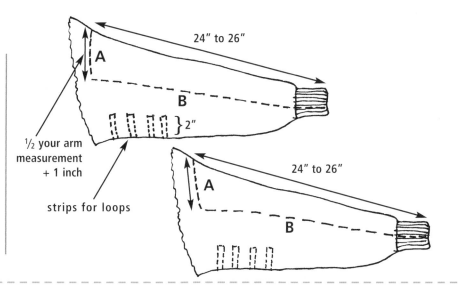

2. Lay cut sleeve pieces flat with right sides facing up. Position eight fabric strips/loops on each sleeve, at least 1 inch from raw edges, keeping loops aligned and evenly spaced, as shown. Position first two loops just above ribbing, and next and subsequent rows 2 inches apart. Pin in place, then stitch loops to sleeves ¼ inch from top and bottom edges of loops, in direction indicated by arrows.

3. With right sides facing, fold armwarmers in half lengthwise; pin. Stitch underarm seams down entire length, including ribbing.

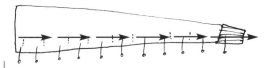

4. Turn armwarmers right side out. Beginning at shoulder end, thread ribbons through loops in crisscross fashion, as shown. Tie ribbons in bows at wrist.

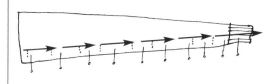

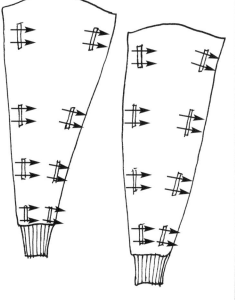

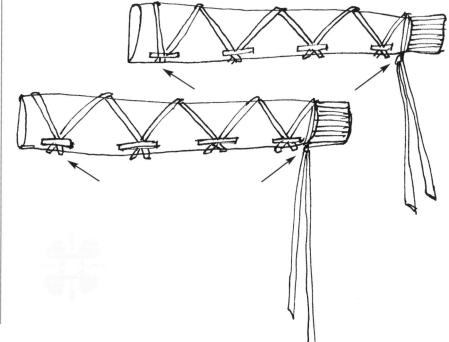

flower brooch with rhinestone center

SKILL LEVEL: 1

REQUIRED TIME:

BY MACHINE AND
HAND BOTH:
1 ½ HOURS

Just when you thought flowers grew only in the garden, they bloom here in frumpy sweat fabric. This elegant flower brooch was made from vintage gray sweat fabric and adorned with a rhinestone center and gunmetal leather petals, topstitched in white. Wear atop a blazer or an array of blouses; sport it on your favorite purse or as a pendant on a chain. It reminds me of the vintage earrings my mother wore to her prom in the '60s. You need very little material to create this dynamic piece.

Materials

STANDARD MATERIALS

Fabric scissors

Marking devices

Measuring devices

Quilting straight pins (or other heavy-duty straight pins)

Thread in matching or contrasting color

Iron and ironing board

Sewing machine and sewing machine needles (optional)

Handsewing needles

SPECIAL MATERIALS

Two felt scraps, each at least 4 inches by 6 inches

Three sweatshirt scraps, each at least 16 inches by 16 inches

Leather scrap, 4 ½ inches by 6 inches

Rhinestones or recycled jewelry for flower center

Pin back (premade pin for back of brooch; available at craft stores)

Protractor to draw circle (or use lid, glass, cup, etc.)

Fabric glue (We recommend Aleene's fabric glue.)

Cardboard, wax paper, plastic, or other nonporous material,
   to act as a barrier to the glue

page 20) at each end of strip to further secure. Pin in place.

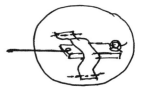

4. Take one 16-inch–by–16-inch sweatshirt scrap. Fold in half, then in half again to make 4-inch–by–4-inch piece. Mark flower petal design, remembering that design represents one-fourth of flower.

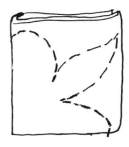

5. Cut out flower along marked petal lines through all fabric layers; unfold when cut. Put aside.

1. Lay two 4 1/2-inch–by–6-inch pieces of felt flat, on top of one another, with wrong sides facing up. Using marking device, trace 3 1/2-inch diameter circle and mark 1/2-inch–by–2 1/2-inch strip onto top piece. Using fabric scissors, cut out circle and strip, through both fabric layers. Put one circle aside; you'll use in Step 8.

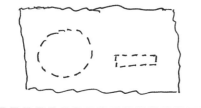

2. Take one circle and lay flat, right side up. Center pin back on circle; glue in place.

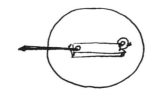

3. Open pin. Lay felt strip cut in Step 1 over base of pin back, keeping pin free, as shown. Glue strip snugly in place. When glue dries, topstitch (see page 19) or whipstitch (see

6. Repeat Steps 4 and 5 on the other two sweatshirt scraps, but vary flower petal design and slightly reduce size. Put aside.

7. Lay 4-inch–by–6-inch leather scrap flat. Mark two or three leaf shapes, same size or various sizes, on wrong side; cut out. NOTE: You can also use denim, wool, tweed, Ultrasuede, or suede for leaves.

8. To assemble flower, lay felt circle *without* pin flat with right side facing up. Lay large flower on circle. Layer one smaller flower over large flower. Topstitch flower layers to circle through center of petals, or glue in place, then tack with hand stitch when glue is dry (B).

Arrange leaves, sliding under petals. Glue leaves in place and allow to dry. Hand tack to further secure (C).

Place third flower in center and topstitch, or glue and hand tack, in place. Add embellishments to center of flower. We used an old rhinestone earring, sewn on by hand. Use crystals, buttons, sequins, rhinestones, or decorative beads as desired (D).

9. Turn flower over and glue felt pin back made previously to wrong side of circle, forming base of flower. When glue is dry, whipstitch edges of circles, as shown, to further secure.

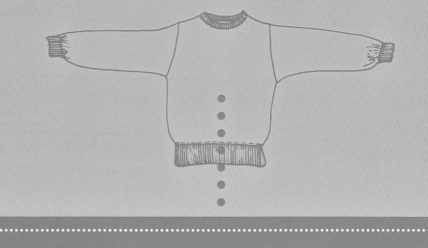

Couture

TOTALLY AND UNEXPECTEDLY,
SWEATSHIRTS CAN BE TRANSFORMED
INTO COUTURE PIECES THAT LOOK AS
IF THEY CAME STRAIGHT FROM THE
ATELIER. THESE UPSCALE STYLES
CAN TRANSFER EFFORTLESSLY FROM
THE STREET TO THE CATWALK.

two-piece tailored sweat suit

This two-piece tailored sweat suit will be your go-to haute couture track-suit! The amazing thing about this design is that you can wear the pieces separately as well as together. The sweat blazer with embellished lapels is a perfect layering piece in colder temperatures, adding panache to any ensemble. The playful ties on the back help define your waistline. The pegged jodhpur pant is comfortably chic. Wear them alone with a variety of casual tops or as a complete suit. Either way, you will look stellar.

Materials

STANDARD MATERIALS

Fabric scissors

Marking devices

Measuring devices

Quilting straight pins (or other heavy-duty straight pins)

Thread in matching or contrasting color

Iron and ironing board

Sewing machine and sewing machine needles (optional)

Handsewing needles

SPECIAL MATERIALS

One zip-front hoodie sweatshirt with front pocket, your size

One pair matching sweatpants, with or without lower leg zippers
or Velcro closings, one size larger than you wear

(Can be separates or suit. If you can find a zip-front sweat with
a flat collar, you can skip the steps on making the collar.)

Fabric glue (We recommend Aleene's Fabric Glue.)

Cardboard, wax paper, plastic, or other nonporous material,
to act as a barrier to glue

Embellishments of your choice

Pants

1. Using iron, press hoodie and sweatpants. Put hoodie aside. Lay pants flat, right side out with front facing up. Using body measurements (see page 8) and marking and measuring tools (see page 12), mark cutting lines as shown:

A (full calf width) = half calf width (average: 7 to 8 inches) across pant legs from side seam; 6 1/2 to 8 inches up from pant hem

B (fitted calf piece for jodhpur) = half calf width at top (A) end; half lower calf width at bottom (C) end; 6 1/2 to 8 inches long (from A to C)

C (lower calf width) = half lower calf width (average 6 1/2 inches)

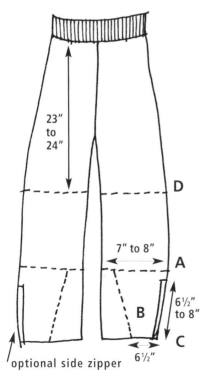

23" to 24"

7" to 8"   A
B   6 1/2" to 8"
C   6 1/2"

optional side zipper

D   D

D (mid-knee) = 23 to 24 inches down from waistband ribbing

Mark cutting lines at mid-knee (D), top of fitted calf piece (A), bottom of leg (C), and side seam (diagonal line) from A to C, as shown. Using fabric scissors, cut along all cutting lines through all fabric layers. Save all remaining sweatpant pieces; you'll use later.

2. Take pants and, using seam ripper or small/embroidery scissors, remove entire inner leg seam, from hem to hem. Leave front and back crotch seam intact.

3. Measure front and back crotch lengths: front length is distance from belly button to crotch (where the front and back center seams and inside leg seams meet on pants); back length is distance from center back waist to crotch. For most people, the front crotch will be 12 to 14 inches; the back crotch will be 14 to 16 inches.

Redraw inner leg seams as follows: Turn pants wrong side out and lay flat with back facing up. Mark back crotch length point on

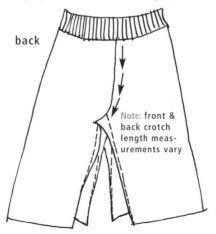

back

Note: front & back crotch length measurements vary

center back/crotch seam line of sweatpants. Turn pants over with front facing up; mark front crotch length point on center front/crotch seam. Redraw front and back inseam (inside leg) cutting lines from crotch to hemlines, as shown.

Cut along new inseam cutting lines through all fabric layers.

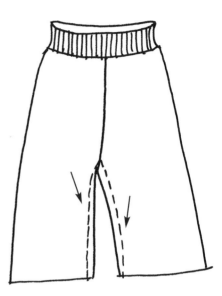

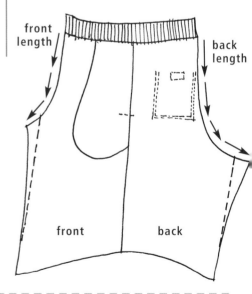

front length

back length

front   back

4. With right sides facing, pin front legs to back legs at inseams, as shown. Stitch seams in direction indicated by arrows. Press inseam seam open and flat.

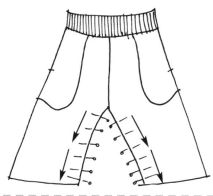

5. With pants still wrong side out, baste (see pages 15 and 16) across bottom of legs, ½ inch from raw edge (A). Pull basting thread in drawstring manner to gather (see page 16) legs, no tighter than full calf measurement (B).

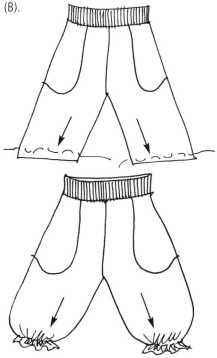

6. Use calf pieces cut in Step 1. Turn wrong side out with right sides facing. Pin at side seams (diagonal cutting lines), as shown, then stitch seams in direction indicated by arrows. Leave sides with vents as is (i.e., open). Press side seam open and flat.

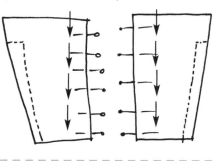

7. Turn pants right side out and lay flat with front facing up. Turn calf pieces wrong side out. Slide calf pieces over pant legs (A) with right sides facing. Slide calf pieces up leg, so bottom edge of calf piece is even with bottom

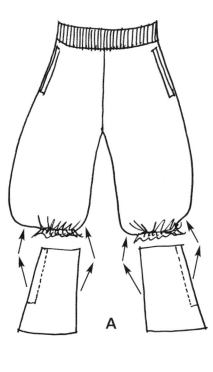

gathered edge of pant (B). Stitch bottom edges together in direction indicated by arrows, stretching calf leg pieces as you sew. (Do not pin calf pieces to leg; it makes seam harder to stitch.) Press seams open and flat.

Fold calf pieces down and right side out (C).

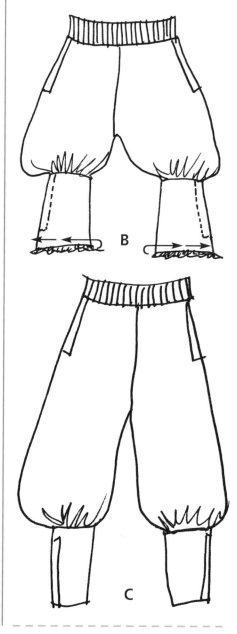

Jacket

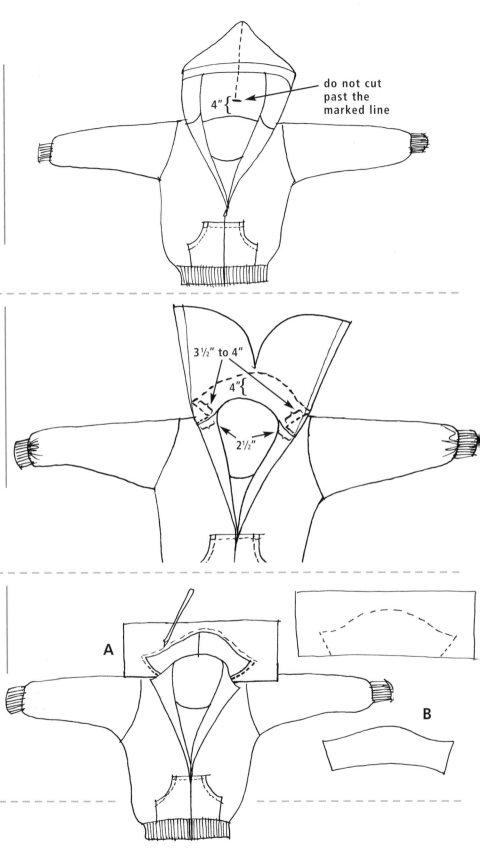

8. Lay hoodie flat, right side out with front facing up. Cut down center of hood, from front of hood to 4 inches *above* base of hood/back neckline.

do not cut past the marked line

4"

9. Mark cutting lines for collar and lapels as follows: At center front, mark a point 2 1/2 inches in along hood/neck seam line, just above neckline, and draw an angled line up from point as shown (lapel width). Beginning at this point, mark curved cutting line for collar around neckline, 4 inches from neckline. (You can trim collar to 3 1/2 inches at ends of collar, if desired.) Carefully cut along all lapel and collar cutting lines as shown. (Cut lapels *above* neckline seam.)

3½" to 4"

4"

2½"

10. Lay flat, as before. Select leftover fabric piece that is longer and wider than the jacket collar. Place fabric piece under jacket collar and trace around collar onto fabric piece (A). Remove fabric piece and cut along marked lines (B). This is the top collar.

A

B

11. With hoodie right side out and front facing up, lay top collar under jacket collar, so right side of top collar is facing in; pin around top and side edges, stopping ½ inch from neckline/lapel on side edges of collar. DO NOT PIN BOTTOM (NECKLINE) *edges of collar and top collar.* Stitch seam beginning and ending ½ inch from neckline/lapel on side edges of collar. (Do not stitch collar to under collar along neckline edges.) Trim corners and seams, and press seams flat.

Turn jacket over so back is facing up. On top collar, turn bottom raw edge (neckline edge) under ½ inch and press.

Turn collar right side out (top collar will turn over to the front side) and press. Pin folded neckline edge of turned collar to neckline seam of hoodie. Whipstitch (see page 20) folded edge of collar to hoodie neckline seam for clean finish.

13. For back ties, cut two 2-inch–by–20-inch strips from pants scraps. Turn jacket right side out and lay flat with back facing up. Mark center back at waist, then measure out 2 to 2½ inches on each side of center back waist (on average, 15 to 17 inches down from center back neck) and mark. With right sides facing, pin 2-inch edge of each strip to each side mark on jacket back only, then stitch ties to jacket back in direction indicated by arrows.

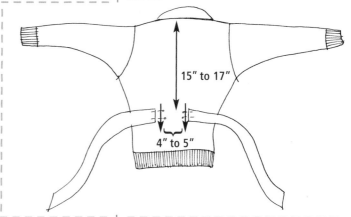

leave under collar space open

12. Fold right-side-out hoodie in half along center front, matching collar, armhole, side seams, and sleeves. Mark side seam cutting line so jacket will be fitted at bust, waist, and hip, but not too tight. Mark underarm cutting line on sleeve so that upper sleeve = shoulder/armpit circumference, plus 2 inches; and sleeve at elbow = elbow circumference, plus 2 inches, on average 5 to 6 inches (A). Cut along all cutting lines through all fabric layers.

Turn jacket wrong side out and lay flat. Pin side and underarm seams, then stitch in direction indicated by arrows (B).

14. Fold ties over stitching lines, so wrong side of tie is facing right side of jacket back. Topstitch (see page 19) across tie in direction indicated by arrows, ¼ inch from previous stitching line, as shown.

Decorate front lapels with topstitching, embellishments, and accessories, as desired.

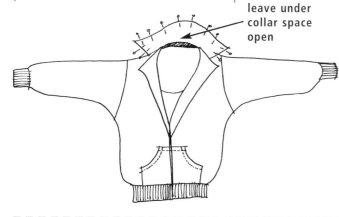

A
your measurement +2"
5" to 6"
depending on your arm measurement

B

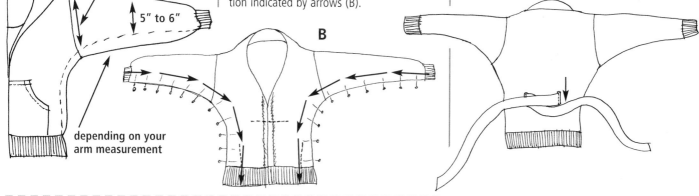

hooded poncho with leather tassels

SKILL LEVEL: 4

REQUIRED TIME:

BY MACHINE:

3 HOURS

BY HAND:

5 HOURS

S weats have come a long way, baby. The sweat evolution takes a giant leap forward with this hooded poncho. It's made in charcoal gray sweat fabric with similarly toned pewter leather trim and tassels for monochromatic sophistication. The leather can be swapped for tassels made of denim, T-shirt, sweatshirt, cord, or any trim you desire. Dress it up or down. You are the ultimate designer!

Materials

STANDARD MATERIALS

Fabric scissors

Marking devices

Measuring devices

Quilting straight pins (or other heavy-duty straight pins)

Thread in matching or contrasting color

Iron and ironing board

Sewing machine and sewing machine needles (optional)

Handsewing needles

SPECIAL MATERIALS

One zip-front hoodie sweatshirt, size L to XL

One crew-neck sweatshirt, size L to XL, in same color as hoodie

Leather, 14 inches by 20 inches, makes 40 tassels
    (use larger piece if more tassels are desired)

Leather scraps for hand vent corners

Fabric glue (We recommend Aleene's Fabric Glue)

Cardboard, wax paper, plastic, or other nonporous material,
    to act as a barrier to the glue

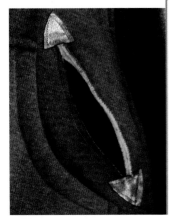

1. Press hoodie, then lay flat, right side out with front facing up. Using measuring and marking devices, mark cutting lines (see page 12) on each side of bodice, beginning 4½ inches in from armhole seam at shoulder, to top of hem ribbing at side seam, then down ribbing to bottom edge, as shown. Using fabric scissors, cut along both cutting lines through all fabric thicknesses. This is piece A.

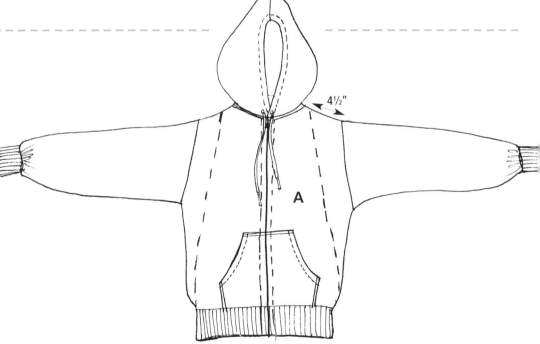

4½"

A

2. Open hoodie piece A and fold in half lengthwise with wrong sides facing, along center front and center back, matching side and ribbing edges. On front of A mark 5½-inch diagonal cutting line for hand vent slit 3 inches from curved opening of pocket, as shown. Also mark ³⁄₈ inches across at top and bottom of slit, perpendicular to slit. Cut along 5½-inch and ³⁄₈-inch cutting lines through both fabric layers. These will become hand vents.

3. Press crew-neck sweatshirt. With right side out, lay flat and fold along center front, matching armholes, side seams, and sleeves. Mark curved cutting line as shown, beginning ½ inch below center front neck, curving gently to side seam at top of ribbing, then down ribbing to bottom. Cut along marked line through all fabric layers. These are two B pieces.

4. Open piece A and lay flat with right side facing up. NOTE: Front and back are joined at shoulder seams.

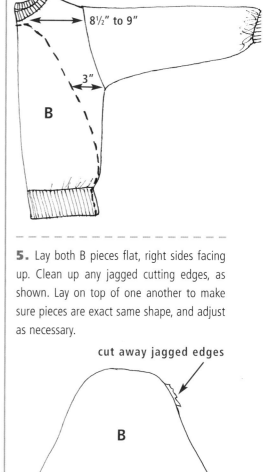

5. Lay both B pieces flat, right sides facing up. Clean up any jagged cutting edges, as shown. Lay on top of one another to make sure pieces are exact same shape, and adjust as necessary.

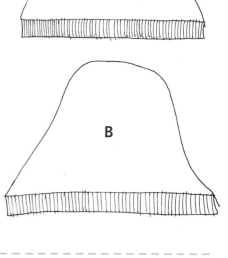

cut away jagged edges

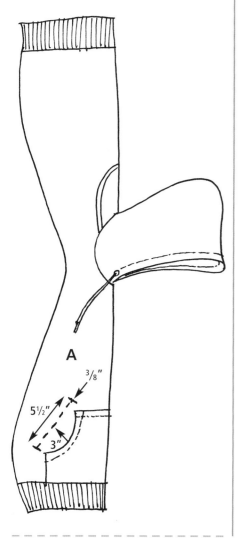

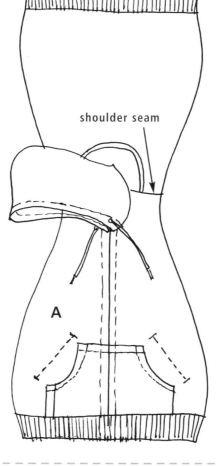

shoulder seam

6. Lay one B piece on top of open, flat A piece with right sides facing. Match center top of piece B to shoulder seam of piece A, then pin B to A at center and 1½ inches each side of center. Stitch 3-inch-long seam and remove pins. With right sides facing, pin remainder of piece B to piece A, matching ribbing and easing B piece into curved edges of A piece, as shown. Clip edges as necessary to make smooth fit. Stitch seam in direction indicated by arrows. Clip curves and press seams flat.

- -

7. Repeat Step 6 on opposite side.

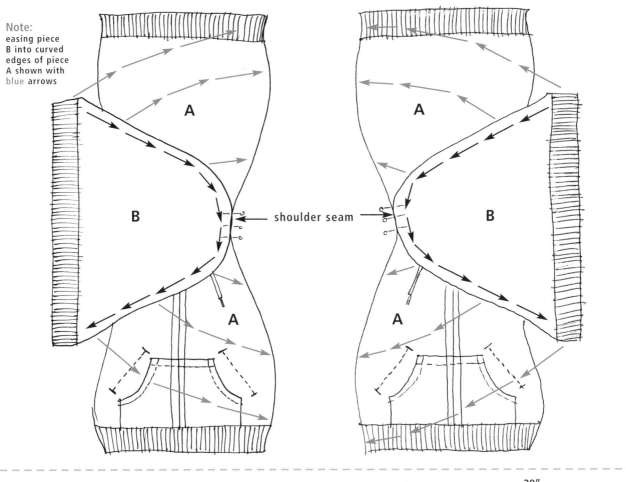

Note: easing piece B into curved edges of piece A shown with blue arrows

shoulder seam

8. Using leather scraps, mark (on wrong side) and cut out four ½-inch arrowhead (triangle) shapes (C) for hand vent corners. Put aside; you will use in Step 12.

- - - - - - - - - - - - - - -

9. Using leather piece, mark (on wrong side) and cut out forty to eighty ½-inch–by–14-inch strips (D). Put aside; you will use in Step 12.

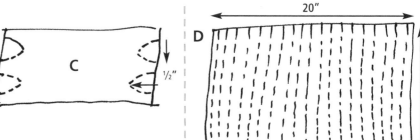

C

½"

20"

D

14"

½"

10. Turn poncho right side out and lay flat with front facing up. Mark buttonhole placements (see pages 20 and 21) around ribbing, $1\frac{1}{2}$ inches from hemline. Mark ten to twenty $\frac{1}{2}$-inch buttonholes on front, then turn over and mark ten to twenty $\frac{1}{2}$-inch buttonholes on back. Number of buttonholes equals number of tassels desired. Stitch buttonholes, then cut open buttonholes.

NOTE: If you don't have a buttonholer on your machine, you can get buttonholes made at your local dry cleaner. For a no-sew method, just cut $\frac{1}{2}$-inch slits at buttonhole markings, sealing the edges with fabric glue or Fray Check.

11. To finish hand vents, lay poncho flat, right side out with front facing up. Fold under $\frac{1}{4}$ inch of edges of slits (cut in Step 2) to wrong side; topstitch (see page 19) $\frac{1}{8}$ inch from folded edge, in direction indicated by arrows.

12. Take four arrowhead pieces (C) and, using fabric glue, glue one at each end of hand vents. Allow glue to dry, then topstitch (see page 19) $\frac{1}{8}$ inch away from outside edges.

Slip two leather strips (D), through each buttonhole. Knot four ends of strips just below hemline; four fringes dangle from each buttonhole. (Optional: String beads onto strips before knotting.)

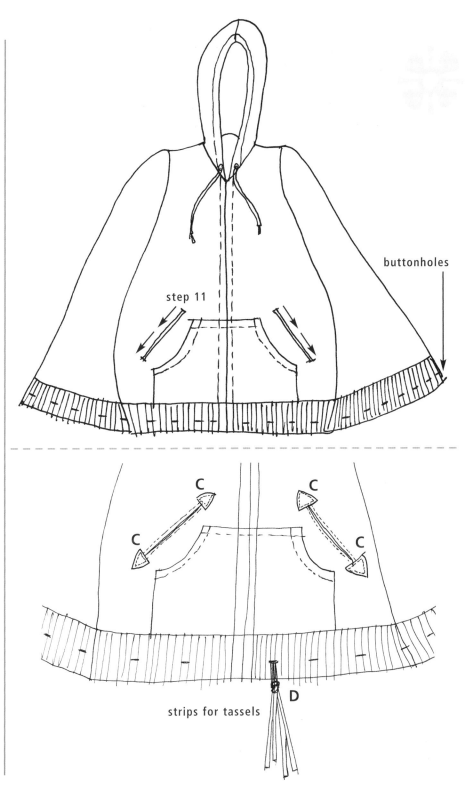

buttonholes

step 11

strips for tassels

glossary

ACCENT—emphasis or prominence given to a line or decorative color in clothing or costume

A-LINE—slightly flared from the waist or shoulders

APPLIQUÉ—decoration laid and applied to another surface; ornamentation applied to a piece of material

AWL—a pointed tool used for making holes in leather, fabric, or wood

BACKSTITCH—an overlapping hand stitch made by starting next stitch at middle of preceding one; used for strength in plain sewing and embroidery

BASTE—to make a series of long, widely spaced straight stitches by hand or machine to temporarily hold two or more layers of fabric together or to mark a stitching line; also used for gathering

BIAS—the direction of a piece of woven fabric, usually referred to simply as "the bias"; bias runs at 45° angle to its warp (straight grain line) and weft (cross grain line) threads

BIAS TAPE—a narrow strip of fabric, cut on the bias, used in piping, binding seams, finishing raw edges, and as decorative detail; varies in width from ½" to 3 inches. The bias cut gives bias tape four-way stretch, and makes it more fluid and easier to drape than a fabric strip that is cut on the straight or cross grain lines. Bias cuts lay smoothly across curves and straight edges alike. Many strips can be pieced together into a long "tape."

BODICE—the torso part of a shirt or dress that extends from the waist to the shoulder and around the body

BOBBIN—a thread holder that feeds the bottom thread in machine sewing. Housed in a bobbin case, it lies directly under the metal plate beneath the presser foot that holds the fabric in place while you sew.

CARE LABEL—a required label in which manufacturers and importers provide at least one satisfactory method of care necessary for the ordinary use of the garment. Most labels include fabric, content, cleaning, and ironing instructions, and the region where the garment was made.

CENTER BACK FOLD (C.B.F.)—the exact (vertical) middle line on the back of a garment or garment part. To determine C.B.F., fold the garment in half lengthwise, with the back side facing up; the fold line is the C.B.F.

CENTER FRONT FOLD (C.F.F.)—the exact (vertical) middle line on the front of a garment or garment part. To determine C.F.F., fold the garment in half lengthwise, with the front side facing up; the fold line is the C.F.F.

COUTURE—French word meaning "sewing" or "needlework"; the business of designing, making, and selling highly fashionable, custom-made, clothing for women; the high-fashion clothing created by designers

CROSS GRAIN—fabric threads that run perpendicular to selvage edge of fabric

CUMMERBUND—a broad fitted sash that fits around the waist, generally pleated

CUT—the style and manner in which a garment is cut and made; the fit of a garment; to make or fashion by cutting with scissors

CUTTING LINE (cutting path)— a line that you follow when cutting out garment and other fabric pieces

DECONSTRUCTION—taking apart an existing garment, accessory, etc., and transforming it into something else (e.g., an old tie becomes a belt, a T-shirt becomes a halter or skirt, a T-shirt becomes a skirt, etc.).

DISAPPEARING INK MARKER—a marking device used on fabric that completely vanishes after a certain amount of time, with or without washing in cold water

DOMESTIC SEWING MACHINE— a sewing machine used at home for personal sewing projects

DRAWSTRING—string, cording, rope, ribbon, etc., running through a fabric tunnel or channel, which when pulled draws the fabric into a tighter gather

DRESSMAKER'S TRACING PAPER— tracing paper designed specifically for fabrics and sewing because the ink easily washes and/or irons out; used with a tracing wheel to mark and transfer cutting and sewing lines, design details, and other sewing guides to fabrics (or to paper patterns)

DRESSMAKER'S TRACING WHEEL— a toothed wheel with a handle that is used with dressmaker's tracing paper

EMBELLISHMENTS—adornments, decorative items added to a garment for style appeal, such as sequins, jewels, trims, appliqués, etc.

EMPIRE WAIST—a high waistline, at or just under the bustline

EMBROIDERY THREAD—thread manufactured or hand-spun specifically for embroidery and other forms of needlework; can be used in single or multiple strands

EYELET—a small hole or perforation usually rimmed with metal, cord, fabric, or leather; used to reinforce a hole; can be decorative or functional

FABRIC GLUE— an adhesive used specially for fabric that is long lasting through laundering and is not stiff when it dries

FASTENER—a device that fastens or holds together separate fabric parts, such as buttons, snaps, and hooks and eyes

FINDINGS—the thread, tapes, buttons, seam or bias binding, hooks and eyes, zippers or slide fasteners, and other sewing essentials used in garment making

FLEECE—synthetic or wool fabric with a soft, silky pile that provides warmth

FRAY—to wear away (the edges of fabric, for example) by rubbing; a threadbare spot as on fabric

FUSIBLE HEMMING TAPE—adhesive strip ½" inch wide, used for hemming; applied at the fold of a garment for a quick hem

GATHER(ING)—to draw up fabric by machine or hand to create fullness

GRAIN—direction in which the threads in fabric run. Straight grain is the long grain running parallel to the selvage and has little or no stretch; the cross grain runs perpendicular to the straight grain and selvage, and has a fair amount of stretch. The bias (running at a 45° angle to straight and cross grains) provides the most stretch

GROMMET—metal eyelet, inserted into cloth or leather, through which a fastener may be passed.

HAND—the texture or feel of cloth (softness coarseness, etc.)

HANDSEWING NEEDLES—needles that come sized in various lengths and thicknesses; different sizes work with different types of fabrics. Handsewing needles are named according to their purpose, such as: sharps, betweens, ballpoint, embroidery, leather, beading, chenille, upholstery, darning, and tapestry

HARDWARE—metal goods used in garments, such as buckles, studs, grommets, etc.

HEM—the fabric at the bottom of a garment or sleeve that is folded to the wrong side (skirt, pant, and dress hems are usually 2 inches; sleeve hems, 1 to 1½" inches)

HEMLINE—the finished length of a garment or sleeve; the line where you fold the fabric to the wrong side to make the hem

HOOK AND EYE—a type of fastener in two pieces—a hook and a loop—which link together to secure the openings on garments

HOODIE—a sweatshirt (zip-front or pullover) with attached hood and usually a front pocket

INSEAM—the inner leg seam of pants that runs from the crotch to the hem

INTERFACING—a moderately stiff/firm material used between layers of fabric to reinforce the fabric; often used in collars, lapels, cuffs, button and zipper plackets, and on the bodice of jackets

IRON—a metal appliance with a handle and a weighted flat bottom; when heated, used to press wrinkles from fabric

IRONING BOARD—a long, narrow padded board, often with collapsible supporting legs, used as a working surface for ironing

MARK—to draw on fabric with tailor's chalk, pen or pencil, or with dressmaker's tracing paper, illustrating where the fabric is going to be cut or stitched; also indicates measurements and waist, bust, hip, and center lines

MEASURE—the act of measuring body parts, fabric pieces, and construction details; to mark, lay out, or establish dimensions by measuring

MONOCHROMATIC—containing or using one color scheme (for example: different shades of the same color (burgundy/red/fuchsia/pink/pastel pink)

NOTCH(ES)—an indentation or incision on an edge, used to indicate where to cut, sew, or fold fabric

PAILLETTES—similar to sequins but larger; used to embellish and adorn garments

PATTERN DRAFTING RULER (A.K.A. QUILTER'S RULER)—a wide, transparent plastic ruler often used for pattern drafting and marking fabric

PIN—to join fabric layers together by running a pin in and out through fabric layers

PINK—to trim edge or cut with pinking shears

PINKING SHEARS—scissors with notched blades, used to finish cut edges of cloth with a zigzag cut for decoration or to prevent raveling or fraying

PRESS—to use a hot iron with plenty of steam to flatten open seams and stitching, and to remove wrinkles from fabrics; the key to easier sewing and fabulous tailoring (use "cotton" or highest heat setting for pressing sweatshirts)

RAW EDGE—unfinished seam or edge of fabric

RIBBING—raised rows of fabric arranged vertically or horizontally

RUFFLES—a strip of frilled or closely gathered fabric used for trimming or decoration

SCISSORS—sharp, long-bladed implement designed to cut fabric

SELVAGE—the reinforced straight grain edges of manufactured fabric

SASH—an ornamental band, scarf, strip, or belt worn around the waist or over the shoulders

SEAM—the joining line where parts of a garment are sewn together

SEAM ALLOWANCE—the distance between the seam line (stitching line) that joins two or more pieces of fabric together and the cut edge of the fabric

SEAM RIPPER—a small device with a small, sharp hook used to remove stitches from any seam

SECURE STITCH—backstitches used to secure hand or machine stitching; alternative to knotting threads

SEQUIN(S)—light-refracting, disk-shaped embellishments used for decorative purposes; either glued or hand sewn on

SILHOUETTE—the shape or outline of the natural body; the shape or outline of the garment

STITCH—a single turn or loop of the yarn or thread, in hand or machine sewing

STITCHING LINE—actual line that you stitch (sew) on

STRAIGHT GRAIN—fabric threads that run parallel to the selvage edge

STRAIGHT PIN—a short, straight stiff piece of metal with a pointed end; used to fasten layers of cloth together before stitching

SWEATSHIRT—loose, long-sleeve, crew-neck pullover of soft, absorbent knit fabric, such as cotton jersey, with close-fitting ribbing at hem, neck, and sleeve cuffs, and ribbing or drawstring at waist; variations include hoodies or zip-fronts

TAILOR'S CHALK—comes in clay, wax, or crayon forms; used for marking on fabric to indicate cutting line, measurements, etc. (clay brushes out of fabric, whereas wax and crayon melt off with a hot, dry iron)

TAPE MEASURE—a length of cloth or plastic tape, 60 inches long, marked at $\frac{1}{8}$ inch intervals; flexible tape hugs body curves when measuring

TOPSTITCH—line of stitches on the face of a garment or along a seam; can be a decorative stitch

TRACING PAPER —semitransparent paper used for tracing and transferring designs, shapes, etc., to fabrics and garment pieces

TRACKSUIT—a sweatshirt, usually a long-sleeve zip-front, and matching sweatpants, traditionally worn by athletes before and after workouts and competitions

WHIPSTITCH—short, easy, hand stitch used to join two finished edges, where the stitches pass over the raw edges diagonally; not an invisible stitch—often decorative

ZIGZAG STITCH—a chain stitch made by inserting a needle at an angle and alternating from side to side; looks similar to inverted letter z

ZIPPER—a fastening device consisting of parallel rows of metal, plastic, or nylon teeth on adjacent edges of an opening that are interlocked by a sliding tab

ZIPPER FOOT—a sewing machine attachment used when sewing on a zipper

VISUAL GLOSSARY
skirts

Bubble skirt Wrap skirt Asymmetrical skirt Pencil skirt

Peasant skirt Ruffle flared skirt Mini skirt A-line skirt

sleeve types

Puffed sleeve
Puffed cap sleeve
Cap sleeve
Ruffled cap sleeve

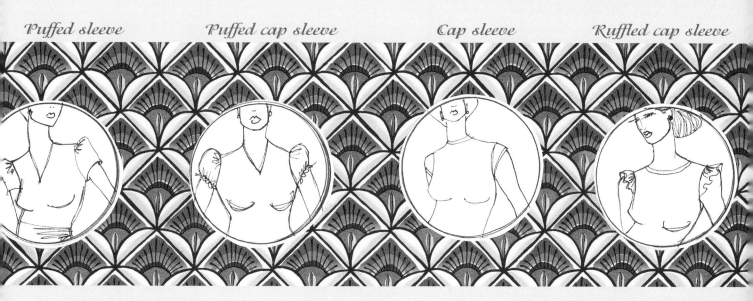

Raglan Sleeve
Bell sleeve
Kimono sleeve
Bishop sleeve

CREDITS

PHOTOGRAPHY—DERRICK GOMEZ,
  WWW.DERRICKGOMEZ.COM
HAIR—DANA GIBBS, WWW.DANASLOFT.COM
MAKEUP—SHADÉ BOYEWA-OSBORNE
CAMERA ASSISTANT—ORLANDO CANTOR
GAFFER—NAT AGUILAR
BEST BOY/ELECTRIC GRIP—ANDREW RODDEWIG
STYLIST ASSISTANT—JOSELYN HARMON
ACCESSORIES
ALEXIS BITTAR, WWW.ALEXISBITTAR.COM
KIMI WEAR, WWW.KIMIWEAR.COM
KIMINA BAYLLI, WWW.BAYLLI.COM
MESH, WWW.MESHNY.COM

VIDHSEL VS LLIAM,
  WWW.MYSPACE.COM/VIDHSELVSLLIAM
ALL CLOTHING SISTAHS OF HARLEM EXCEPT BLACK
  MAXI SKIRT FROM SOHUNG DESIGNS,
  WWW.SOHUNGDESIGNS.COM
MODELS
CONSUELO @ MAJOR MODEL MANAGEMENT,
  WWW.MAJORMODELMANAGEMENT.COM
MYA (FREELANCE)
NIA REED @ IMAGES MANAGEMENT,
  WWW.IMAGESNYC.COM
TONI @ ID MODEL MANAGEMENT,
  WWW.IDMODELS.COM

RESOURCES

SWEATS
LOCAL SOURCES:
  SALVATION ARMY, GOODWILL OR OTHER
  THRIFT STORES
  FAMILY OR FRIEND'S CLOSETS
  YOUR CLOSET
  FLEA MARKETS
  CHURCH SECONDHAND SALES
  SWAP PARTIES WITH FRIENDS
  YARD SALES
  VINTAGE BOUTIQUES
ONLINE SOURCES:
  WWW.EBAY.COM
  WWW.CHAMPIONCATALOG.COM
  WWW.CHEAPESTEES.COM
  WWW.LLBEAN.COM
  WWW.AMERICANAPPAREL.NET
  WWW.TARGET.COM
  WWW.JIFFYSHIRTS.COM

RIBBONS AND TRIMS
  WWW.MJTRIM.COM
  WWW.FASHIONFABRICSONLINE.COM
  WWW.DISTINCTIVEFABRIC.COM
  WWW.GALAXYTRIM.COM

WWW.FABRIC.COM
WWW.EJOYCE.COM

BASIC SEWING AND CRAFT SUPPLIES
  WWW.JOANN.COM
  WWW.SEWTRUE.COM
  WWW.MICHAELS.COM
  WWW.PEARLPAINT.COM

THE ONE-STOP WARDROBE SUPPLY SHOP
  WWW.WARDROBESUPPLIES.COM

EMBELLISHMENTS
  WWW.MYBEDAZZLER.COM
  WWW.GROVEGEAR.COM (FOR PATCHES)
  WWW.GLITZONLINE.COM

LEATHER SCRAPS
  WWW.4HIDES.COM
  WWW.BRETTUNSVILLAGE.COM
  WWW.TWSLEATHER.COM
  WWW.SKINNYLLAMA.COM

WHERE TO FIND US
  WWW.SISTAHSOFHARLEM.COM
  WWW.MYSPACE.COM/SISTAHSOFHARLEM

ACKNOWLEDGMENTS

We are grateful to God and the Universe for the opportunity on this third book. To everyone listed below: Thanks so much for believing in and supporting us. We love you all! **Libbie and Jerry Johnson:** You are truly the gust of wind beneath my wings. Thanks for the love and support. **Cherod and Maurice Webber:** You are my guardian angels. Thanks for everything. **Winston Webber:** Thanks for introducing me to Picasso at a young age and encouraging me as an artist. In loving memory of **Grandma Fannie:** Thanks for being the brilliant woman you are and were. Each stitch represents each year of courage you have granted me as a fashion designer, artist, and writer. **Mama Faye:** Thanks for the amazing stories and exposure to fashion throughout the years. **Uncle Francis and Aunt Nancy Webber:** Thanks for making me feel like a princess, the greatest artist/fashion designer throughout the years. **Betty Marshall:** Without you I would not exist and can not imagine life without you. You are pure sunshine. **Takiyah and Frederick Jackson:** My perfect sister, the voice of reason and my wonderful brother-in-law. Thank you. **Sandra Marshall:** You're amazing, thanks for helping me pursue my dreams. **The entire Jones and Marshall family and friends:** Thanks for believing. **Simone Thomas:** I adore you, cuz! Thanks a million for the years of support. **Auntie Eb and Auntie Bren:** Thanks

so much for being such wonderful supports of wisdom. **To the Matthews Clan:** Thank you all for the support over the years. **David, Jet Black Horse:** Your amazing spirit has been such a beautiful support. I adore you. **Adrienne Ingrum:** We adore you for being the most amazing agent. Thank you for believing in us. **Marta Hallet:** Thanks so very much for opening doors for us with *T-Shirt Makeovers*. **Martha Moran:** You are the most amazing teacher/mentor/editor. We really appreciate all of your hard work. **BJ Berti:** Thank you for the opportunity. **Jasmine Faustino:** Thanks for all of your hard work. **Sony Heron:** Luna Llena Management is brilliant. Thanks so much for supporting us over the years. **Derrick Gomez:** Thanks for being such an amazing photographer and supporting us over the years. **Carmencita Whonder:** Thanks for the unconditional support. I can always depend on you. I wish you lived in NY! **Samiyah Johnson:** You truly are one of the most fabulous, stylish divas in the world. **Jackie Smith:** Thanks for listening and not judging. **Cherisse Bradley:** You are the angel with the amazing voice. **Kimberly Britto-Ukkerd:** The Kimiwear bracelets are practically glued to me. Thanks for being a friend! **Joseph Burton:** Thanks so much for always supporting Sistahs of Harlem and my dreams. **Katrina and Natalie Markoff:** Vosges Haute Chocolates are the

most amazing in the world. Thank you both for continuing to be such brilliant mentors. **Dale Lindholm** of Pure Accessories, N.Y.: Thanks so much for your support over the years. **Joselyn Harmon:** We appreciate your loving support over the years. **N'Dea Davenport:** You're an amazingly fabulous rock star songstress. **Nichelle Sanders:** Thanks so much for the brilliant support through the years. **Audrey Dussards:** Thanks so much for all the years of support. **Leonard Robinson:** Thanks for making me laugh. **Zakiaayah Salim, Latasha Greer, Tiffany Anderson, Jewel Antoine, and Aneska Mitchell:** Thanks for your constant support and constant words of encouragement. They keep me going! **Princess Mhoon Cooper:** I miss you. Thanks for your support. **Erica Sewell and Jasaun Buckner:** I'm glad we've hung out so much over the years, it's been amazing. I look forward to the years to come. **Ali and Francis Bradley:** Ali—We're inspired by your endless energy. Never lose it! **Francis—The mural is hot! I love it! **Anthony Santagati:** So much thanks for your support. You're one of the most reliable people I know! **To all the family and friends not mentioned,** we truly appreciate and love your support over the years. Thank you. We adore you all. And **those we forgot,** please blame the mind and not the heart.

INDEX